How to Keep Your Family Connected

Examples, Stories, Techniques, and Resources

Mitzi Perdue

For Frank Perdue

My late husband wasn't a family-business theoretician, yet he put untold thought, effort, and love into influencing and designing his family's culture. He could have ignored this and left it to chance. The fact that he didn't makes me believe that the admiration he deserves as a successful businessman was at least matched by the admiration he deserves as a successful family man.

How to Keep Your Family Connected
Examples, Stories, Techniques, and Resources

by Mitzi Perdue

Contents

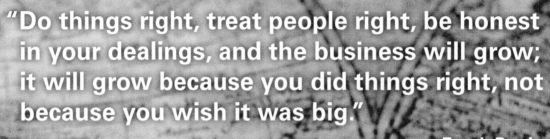

"Do things right, treat people right, be honest in your dealings, and the business will grow; it will grow because you did things right, not because you wish it was big."

—Frank Perdue

What's Needed for Creating and Maintaining a High-Functioning Family?

THE SAD STORY OF THE FAMOUS LAST NAMES CLUB

I had a searing experience a few years ago. I was with a group that called ourselves "The Famous Last Names Club," and all sixteen women who attended had last names that you would instantly recognize. (I wish I could tell you who was there, but honest, I can't because one of the conditions of membership was that we could never reveal each other's names.)

We used to get together over lunch in the private room of a financial institution that loves to cater to high-net-worth clients. The purpose was to talk about issues that confronted us because of our famous last names. One month the topic was, "How well do you get along with your sibling?"

We were sitting around a mahogany conference table, and we went around the table, giving our answers. A woman in her fifties answered first, describing how she and her sisters squabbled over everything, whether money, children, or even who was getting the most attention from their parents.

"The pain of this relationship permeates every hour of every day," she said in words that burned into my memory.

Another woman in her late thirties talked about how her two brothers squeezed her out of the business by not letting her know when the meetings were. She felt miserable and betrayed, and again the pain was unending.

Still another in our group talked about how she felt when her brother took her to court over their father's will. When her brother falsely testified against her, she realized that her brother loved money more than he loved her. She said in the saddest voice you can imagine, "I'm 70, and at this age, when your 80-year-old brother lies about you in court, it's not something that can ever be put back together."

MY EXPERIENCE WAS DIFFERENT

Hearing their stories, I was shocked. Of the sixteen women, only one shared my experience of having a supportive family.

I was the last to answer, and when it came my turn to talk about my relationship with my siblings, it was embarrassing. I knew I was going to come across as Miss Goodie Two Shoes and on top of that, I didn't want to make them feel bad by showcasing how different my experience had been.

What I could have said was, "The best part of my life is my relationship with my family, and my relationship with my siblings is the best part of that!"

What I did say was, "Mumble, mumble, mumble, mumble my experience doesn't match yours, but each family is different."

Nobody followed up on my non-responsive answer. Still, the whole conversation made me realize yet again that, yes, failing family relationships are everywhere and they're unmercifully painful.

The experience reminded me of something I had recently read. Relationship problems are the reason that 70% of families don't make it to the next generation.[1]

The lunch ended and I was left wondering why it was that the two families I'm closest to are so different from what seems to be the norm. My family of origin is

---

1. Roy Williams and Vic Preisser, *Preparing Heirs: Five Steps to a Successful Transition of Family Wealth and Values*, p. 17 (San Francisco: Robert D. Reed Publishers, 2003).

the Henderson family, and we began in 1890 with the Henderson Estate Company. This was the forerunner of the Sheraton Hotels, which my father co-founded. We're about to have our 127th reunion, and in surveys, family members often say that the family reunions are the most joyous and meaningful parts of their lives.

My family by marriage is the Perdue family, and the Perdues have been getting together regularly since Perdue Farms started in 1920. My Perdue family members are not just in-laws, but some of the best friends I'll ever have in life.

I admire them, love them, and both the Henderson and the Perdue families make me think of what Johnny Depp, the movie star, once said: "If someone were to harm my family, I would eat them. I might end up in jail for 500 years, but I would eat them."

I think Johnny Depp had it just about right. If I ever meet him, I want to tell him, "Me too!"

What did the Hendersons and the Perdues do to remain united and high-functioning over a combined period of 224 years?

HOW DO YOU TRANSMIT A CULTURE THAT SUPPORTS A HIGH-FUNCTIONING FAMILY?

When I look at my two families as well as some of the families I've known since childhood, I become ever more convinced that Dr. Robyn Fivush, the Director of the Family Narratives Lab at Emory University, has come across something extraordinarily significant. Her research shows that the culture we create by the stories we tell each other is the key to how we act and how we make sense of the world.

Family stories tell us who we are and how we should act. Our family stories are the bedrock of the family culture.

But how do you tell the stories that bind a family together if there are several generations and they live far apart?

That's the question Frank and I were wrestling with back in 1995.

I remember we were driving from Midlothian, Virginia, where we had been visiting his youngest daughter, Beverly Jennings. It was a four-and-a-half-hour drive, he was at the wheel, and we got to talking about how at 75-years old, he knew so many things about life, things he wanted to transmit to his children and grandchildren. He knew that the stories and precepts would make their lives happier and more fulfilling.

"For example?" I asked.

"They need to understand stewardship and philanthropy. They need to know the importance of frugality and humility and giving back. They need to know that people will be constantly coming to them with 'can't lose' investments. They need to understand that they're part of something bigger than just themselves."

"Why don't you just call them together and tell them these things? My father used to do this with me and my siblings. He'd sit us down in his den and talk to us about what my mother used to call 'recipes for living.'"

Frank thought about this for a moment as we drove through a forested area of Virginia's eastern shore. Then, shaking his head as he continued to drive, he said, "I can't do that. It would feel really awkward."

"But it would be a shame," I answered, "to have your kids and grandkids miss out on information that could help them in their lives. They look up to you. They'd *want* to know."

We drove on in silence for a few minutes. I knew it wasn't in Frank's personality to just stand up and lecture at his children. He was a shy man, and it didn't suit his personality. On top of that, by 1995, his children and grandchildren were spread from Maine to Virginia. We'd have to find something else.

And then it hit me.

THE PERDUE FAMILY NEWSLETTERS

"What about having a newsletter? I could interview you as if I were a reporter. I could ask you stories about your life and the values that you hold dear. Each child or grandchild could get his or her own copy of the newsletter."

Frank immediately loved the idea. We started that weekend, and it was the beginning of something I've been doing for more than two decades.

Newsletters are a perfect way for transmitting your family's culture. Because of these newsletters, Frank's descendants know his views on a vast array of subjects, including such things as prenuptial agreements, career choice, and why living way below your means is a great life strategy.

The first year's newsletters consisted of asking Frank about his stories and what he wanted those who came after him to know. However, the newsletters soon branched out to include interviews with other members of Frank's generation. Some of the aunts and uncles were in their late eighties or nineties, and I felt that if we didn't get their stories about their early lives, we'd lose those stories forever.

And what stories there were! There were family members who, growing up around 1910, lived in a log house where snow blew through the cracks in the logs. They'd have to get up at 5:00 am in an unheated room, and one of them had to milk the cows each day before going to school.

The newsletters soon evolved to include interviews with newly-engaged couples, descriptions of weddings, and a continuing series of interviews with family members about their careers. The newsletters became truly "news and stories" letters as opposed to simply "newsletters."

In writing about what was going on in the family and by telling stories from family members, I had by accident hit on something important. According to Dr. Fivush, high-functioning families are ones whose members know their family stories.

HELP DESIGN YOUR FAMILY CULTURE

It turns out that the stories we tell ourselves are what bind us together. Stories makes us stronger and more resilient.

"We have empirical evidence for this," Dr. Fivush told me in a phone conversation. "Members of these families are better off both physically and psychologically, they do better academically, and they're more satisfied with life."

What better inheritance to pass down

Unfortunately, these high-functioning families are not the norm. As Roy Williams, a family-business advisor from the Williams Group and co-author of *Preparing Heirs: Five Steps to a Successful Transition of Family Wealth and Values* once told me, roughly 70% of family businesses don't make it to the second generation, and only 3% make if to the fourth generation.

The reason for these discouraging figures is that most often the family business didn't have a culture that supported staying together. The fact is every family has a culture but the question is whether the culture is one that came about by accident or by design. The ones that came about by accident and that left values and attitudes to chance rarely support either a high-functioning family life or a family business that stays in the family.

In the ones that failed, often there were quarrels or jealousies, or individuals who felt it was more important to be right than to have a relationship. Their family culture didn't protect them from these toxic attitudes. And as I mentioned earlier, I've witnessed the pain and sadness that accompanies cultures that don't encourage people to realize that they're part of something bigger than themselves.

With your newsletters, you can help design your family's culture so it supports being a high-functioning family. The family culture you help design is like an internal computer software program that lets family members know "This is how we do things." With your newsletters, you can give your family a better chance of being in the 30% that do make it to the next generation.

WHAT WOULD YOU GIVE TO HAVE A HIGH-FUNCTIONING FAMILY?

Wouldn't you like to have a family whose members enjoy and support each other, who are resilient through life's successes and setbacks, and who share positive values centering on "what it means to be us"? Wouldn't you like to encourage a culture of thinking of "us" rather than "I"?

Think about this a moment: The most important task of any generation is to teach the generations that come afterwards how to lead happy and fulfilling lives. With your newsletters, you're taking a major step toward making this happen.

That would be beyond price, right?

The good news is that it can happen And fortunately for members of family businesses, the same factors that make families function well can also help your family business stay in the family.

It gets down to an observation by E.O. Wilson, the Harvard professor who devotes his life to saving wildlife. In the quote you're about to read, he's referring to species, but in your mind, substitute "family" for every time he says, "them."

> The more we know about them, the more we understand them; the more we understand them, the more we care about them; the more we care about them, the more we get to love them. When we love something, it is beautiful and we want to protect it.

That's why, by writing newsletters and telling your family's news and your family's stories, you can do something priceless to help protect and preserve your family across the generations. Communicating with family members on a regular basis can be one of the more important things you do to keep the family together.

YOU'RE NOT A WRITER? NOT TO WORRY!

Ah, that dear friend is precisely why I wrote *How to Strengthen Your Family Legacy with Newsletters*. In this manual, you'll find sample newsletters that you can use for ideas, or in many cases you might simply want to copy the content, substituting appropriate names from your family.

You'll also find lists of questions that go with each newsletter. Pick and choose ones that work best for your situation and answer them. *Voilà*, you've got your own personalized newsletter.

The sample newsletters and sample questions are just a jumping off point for your creativity. But I do have a word of advice: don't hold yourself to a too-high standard at the beginning.

My personal motto is, "Done is better than perfect," and you'll achieve 95% of the goal of writing the newsletter (namely, helping guide and reinforce the family culture) just by having written it. You don't need to be Shakespeare!

At the beginning, just focus on the goal of helping keep your family together by keeping them informed. It's carrying out Wilson's "The more we understand them, the more we care about them."

So, in the immortal words of the Nike slogan, "Just do it!"

HOW DO I USE THE TEMPLATES?

Does composing and formatting a family newsletter seem like a daunting task? I'm sympathetic as can be about this, so I've tried to make it as easy as possible for you.

It will take some effort on your part, but keep in mind that the rewards can be both life-changing and priceless.

So, you're ready to tackle the family newsletter? First, the good news: when you get past the first one, the next will be ten times easier, and each one after that will be easier still.

One thing that should make it easier is that the sample newsletters you'll find here typically are short, and only a few are longer than a couple of pages. You can always make yours longer if you choose, but two pages is easier than a longer newsletter. And, importantly, in today's fast-paced world your family members are more likely to read a short newsletter. They're also more likely to remember and be impacted by a short message than a longer one.

If you're not familiar with formatting mechanics such as cutting and pasting or using drop-down boxes, please, please don't endure the frustration of struggling with this by yourself. (For one thing, I don't want you to hate me, and since I know how exasperating learning new programs can be, I don't want to risk that.)

I said this would take effort, but I don't want it to be unnecessarily hard. Ask your 12-year old nephew (or whomever) to show you any mechanics that you're not familiar with.

So, here's the step-by-step approach to creating your first newsletter:

1. Read through the list of possible newsletter topics.

2. Select the one you want. If you're reading this on a screen, they're hyperlinked. If you're reading the print version, use the good old-fashioned table of contents.

3. Most newsletters will involve an interview. This takes some effort, but it's so worth it because you'll get information that will be lost if someone doesn't record it. There's a real chance that years from now your descendants will be grateful for the record that you're creating. It will be a significant contribution to strengthening the family culture.

4. If you've never conducted an interview, here are a couple of tips. If your family members live nearby, then by all means do the interview in person. Most people doing interviews record them, and there are services on the Internet such as UpWork.com where you can pay people to transcribe interviews for you. Your interview with your family member can be a perfect bonding time for both of you. However, you don't have to do interviews in person. I almost always do interviews by phone, but that's partly because both the Henderson and Perdue families are so spread out. When I start my phone interview, I alert my interviewee that I need them to speak slowly because I'm taking notes as we speak and that I may need to ask him or her to repeat what they just said.

5. When doing the interviews, take advantage of the sample questions in the templates. Some will be totally inappropriate for your situation, but they can help spark your imagination.

6. Be prepared for a learning curve and be patient with yourself the first few times. Doing interviews takes some getting used to, but once you've gotten comfortable with it, this is a skill that will stay with you and you can use many, many times. There's something amazingly special about recording and sharing someone's life, values, knowledge, and experience. You'll be playing a role (even if it's only a small role), in making his or her life more significant. That, by the way, is one of the nicest payoffs for writing newsletters.

7. Using the information from your interview, copy the format of the sample newsletter, substituting your information for what you find in the sample.

8. OK, you've got your newsletter written. It's time for editing. Get a trusted friend to look for typos or parts that aren't clear or are "land mines," where something could be taken the wrong way. I think it's essential to have someone else review it before sending it out.

9. I make it a point to show the final copy to the person I interviewed. Usually they're pleased. But there sure are cases where, with the best intentions, I just

didn't get it right. If they want something changed, I always change it. This is for history and it's got to be right.

10. Distribute it. In my case, I send it out electronically to everyone, but there are also family members who want hard copies, so I use snail mail as well. I also make sure the family archivist has several copies.

11. When you've finished your first one, rejoice. The second one will be easier, and by the time you've been doing them for a year, you'll find that writing a family newsletter can feel like second nature.

By the way, I'm planning on having a fill-in-the blanks template you can use from my website, www.MitziPerdue.com. It will be a drag-and-drop affair where you can pull the information from your interview into a template, and there will also be room for your photographs. You'll be able to distribute your newsletter directly from the website template, using email addresses that you upload just one time.

To sign up for this functionality when it becomes available, e-mail me at mitzi@ mitziperdue.com. I'll put you on the list to get it as soon as it's available. I'd also treasure any advice you have on making the newsletters more useful.

This is a crowd-sourced effort with many people contributing ideas. It's a prime example of "None of us is as smart as all of us."

I have a prediction: I think you'll find that writing these newsletters will become a priceless gift for your family. Newsletters are not going to solve all family problems, but they can go a long way to preventing them. And they can also help your family to be closeer and to care more about each other. They're important deposits in the Bank of Family Closeness.

So let's get started!

"If you want to be happy, think what you can do for someone else. If you want to be miserable, think what's owed to you."

—Frank Perdue

A Family Quarrel? Be Proactive—or Else!

Notes on Using This Newsletter

MOST FAMILY BUSINESSES FAIL TO MAKE IT TO THE NEXT GENERATION. THESE FAILURES almost never come out of the blue. The stresses and strains in family businesses are for the most part predictable, and with nine million family-owned businesses in the United States alone, we know a lot about what those stresses and strains are. In fact, there's a whole academic field devoted to family businesses, and there are some brilliant people devoting their lives to these studies.

Since family quarrels are one of the larger factors in family businesses not making it to the next generation, what can your family do to prevent them?

As you'll see in the following newsletter, I recommend getting help before you need it. My motto on this is, "It wasn't raining when Noah built the Ark!" Establish a relationship with a trusted family-business advisor, and avoid having to reinvent the wheel.

This is an example of the sample texts that you might choose to use as is (with, of course, some input to personalize it). Or, you might choose to begin from scratch, with the sample questions as a way of getting started. I very much hope you do include this topic in one of your newsletters. The stakes couldn't be higher, and a small investment in time and money can prevent untold misery in the future.

PERDUE FAMILY NEWSLETTER

Dearest Family and Family Friends:

This month's newsletter is something of a cautionary tale. There's some downbeat information, but there's a lot that's positive in it as well, and every family member can benefit from knowing the information. It relates to a shocking and sobering statistic from Drew Mendoza, Managing Principal of The Family Business Consulting Group (FBCG).

He told me, "In my 23 years of experience with 2400 clients, I've never seen even one family business that started down the road of litigating with each other that was later able to pull back."

It turns out that if you've started litigation, you've not only crossed a bridge, you've almost certainly blown up the bridge behind you. Reconciliation pretty much doesn't happen once litigation has begun.

By the way, Mendoza knows why families continue down the road of litigation once it's started. "A litigator," he points out, "is employed to do the best for the client. Unfortunately, what's good for the individual client may not be good for the family as a whole or for the family business."

Mendoza's statistic of 0 for 2400 underlies something that we probably already feel in our bones: It's important to intervene early if it looks like a family business quarrel could get out of hand.

In view of Mendoza's long and intense experience with what happens once litigation has begun, he and his 23 colleagues at the FBCG will not take members of family businesses as clients who have initiated litigation. For the kind of service FBCG can provide, by the time a family member is dealing with a litigator, it's too late.

This attitude may seem harsh, but Mendoza and his colleagues have built their reputation around preventing things from getting to this state. They know that even though each family is unique, nevertheless, the challenges and opportunities they each face are normal and predictable. They have the knowledge, tools, and experiences to address these.

The stakes can be extremely high. The happiness of the family and the health of the business are riding on getting this right. Every family business (including ours) needs to put in the effort it takes to get the right advice.

What are the steps Mendoza would recommend to us?

Plan to spend time on this. It's likely to be a long-term relationship spanning generations so it's worth getting it right.

He advises for people who don't already have a family advisor, develop a selection process. He says, "I often encourage people to test drive the consultant by asking the consultant, 'How do you think we ought to go about developing our selection process?'"

Again, for those who don't already have an advisor, plan how the decision will be made. Is it by all members of the family? Is it a selection committee? Is the decision by majority or does it need to be a consensus? Or is our family one where the patriarch or matriarch is the right one to make it?

Some families may want to have the selection committee interview 5 or 6 firms and then winnow it down to 2 or 3, which the selection committee then presents to other family members. When families are still small, it may be enough for one or two family members simply to make the decision.

One of the biggest pain points for any family business is that as many as 70% of them will not be able to pass their wealth and their family business on to the next generation. The most frequent cause for this is family relationships that aren't working out. In this case, we know that being proactive is essential.

Family members can reach Drew Mendoza at the Family Business Consulting Group by e-mailing him at: Mendoza@theFBCG.com Or call him at: 773-604-5005. FBCG's website (www.thefbcg.com) has hundreds of relevant articles and an excellent search engine designed to help families like ours.

Love to all of you,

Sample Questions

Some families have the tradition that it's good to get issues out on the table, even yelling about them if necessary, but no matter what, family members are never to bring in lawyers or the press. Should this apply to our family?

- Do you see any role for litigators in our family relationships?
- What do you see as some of the predictable issues that we as a family business will face?
- Are we prepared for succession issues? Sibling rivalry? Conflict between those who work in the business and those who are stockholders? Voting rights? Roles of family members by blood and by marriage? Divorce? Sale of the company?
- Do we need a family-business advisor?
- How do we go about finding a family-business advisor?
- If we have one, has it been a positive experience?
- What else should we be doing to keep the family together over time?

Where Do We Each Fit In?
A Discussion That Families Need to Have

Notes on Using This Newsletter

I'VE LONG THOUGHT THAT IN BOTH THE IDEAL SOCIETY AND THE IDEAL FAMILY, there's room for everyone and each person is appreciated and valued, whatever their gifts of shortcomings. My ideal family is also egalitarian. There's humility, warmth, caring, and people know they belong and know that they're there for each other.

That's what I think would be ideal. Nobody achieves the ideal, but as poet Robert Browning said, "Man's reach should exceed his grasp" and for me at least it's something to aim for.

Ah, but what happens when an individual family member doesn't feel that she or he belongs? What if the siblings are all going to fabulous colleges and got amazing grades in high school and she didn't? What if it feels like everyone else is amazing, and this child is a normal kid. Where does he or she fit in?

That's a subject worth addressing because, ideally, everyone needs to feel that the family is a place where everyone belongs. I was touched and moved beyond words when a 17-year old step-grandchild raised this question. The act of raising the question meant that it was on its way to being resolved. Is she hadn't brought it up, we couldn't have dealt with it. (As a final note to this story, twenty years later she's popular, adored, effective, and looked up to. Boy, does she fit in! How nice that we could talk about it.)

Does your family have this issue? Is it worth discussing in a newsletter?

PERDUE FAMILY NEWSLETTER

Dearest Family and Family Friends:

This issue has an interview that I think you'll find interesting and thought-provoking. Everyone knows that there are some wonderful advantages to having a famous relative, but there are also some problems with this, and Whitney has had the courage to raise one of them. Bravo, Whitney, for dealing with this head-on!

Love to all of you,

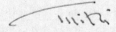

Interview with Whitney Van Der Hyde

Mitzi: Sometimes people in this family wonder if they fit in. Tell me how you feel about it.

Whitney: Because Pops was so successful, I feel that I'm supposed to do something really amazing with my life. I feel that I have to succeed and do something really great, and that means it's hard to be just me. It's even harder because I feel there's a lot of competition among the cousins. Everyone wants to know what college you're going to and what your SAT scores are.

Mitzi: How do you wish it were? What would you change?

Whitney: I feel that the goal should be to fulfill yourself rather than fill someone else's mold. Each person has to think about what really is important to them. Who you are should be more important than what college you go to or how much money you make. Our family ought to embrace that. We each have different gifts and we need to accept that and not just be forced into a standard mold. Like if I wanted to live in a shack in the mountains, that would be okay.

Mitzi: Your mother tells me that having too much competitiveness wasn't much of an issue for her generation. They grew up with the notion that you didn't have to be the best, you just had to do your best.

Whitney: I recognize that if I feel pressure, it may be that I impose some of it on myself, that it's self-generated.

Mitzi: Still, if you feel it, it counts. Talk about how the culture of this family should be.

Whitney: Ideally it would be a place where you come to feel safe and secure and accepted for who you are. The outside world is going to judge you no matter what, and the family should be a place of acceptance and refuge.

Mitzi: I'm so glad you brought all of this up. It will generate thinking and discussion about who we are and who we want to be. Thank you for a tremendous service to the family.

Sample Questions

- Sometimes people in this family wonder if they fit in, true?
- Tell us how you feel about it.
- What kind of change would be helpful to you? How do you wish things were in an ideal world? Is there more competitiveness than you feel comfortable with?
- Do you feel accepted?
- Do you feel too much pressure to perform?
- Do you feel that your particular gifts are valued?
- Do we focus too much on academic success or monetary success?
- How should we measure the worth of each of us?
- Our family has tremendous academic diversity from college graduates to high school dropouts. What can we do to make everyone feel embraced and valued?

Having a Super-Successful Parent:
A Fabulous Legacy or a Painful Impediment?

Notes on Using This Newsletter

WHITNEY VAN DER HYDE RECENTLY ASKED WHERE SHE FIT IN WHEN THERE WAS SO much pressure in our family to be awesome. She felt that there was not enough room left for people to be themselves. This is a tremendously important subject. It gets to the heart of what it means to be a family, since a true family accepts everyone for who they are.

As a member of a family business, you may also come up against the issue of where family members fit in. Is there a founder who's larger than life? Are there family members who forever worry that they're not living up to the awesomeness of the founder?

Literature and the headlines are full of individuals who end up unhappy or have substance-abuse issues or failed marriages or even trouble with the law because they didn't successfully deal with the identity issues that can sometimes accompany having a super-successful relative.

I love it that in the Perdue family, one of the family members was comfortable enough to bring the issue into the open. If this is an issue in your family (or even if you don't know that it is, but think it might be), here's a chance to deal with it. Your family culture will almost certainly handle it with answers that differ from what Frank Perdue said. But his answers can be a springboard to your own family's dealing with this critical issue in your own way.

PERDUE FAMILY NEWSLETTER

Dearest Family and Family Friends:

In the last newsletter, Whitney brought up an extraordinarily important topic: how do we accept that family members have different gifts and yet everyone needs to fit in? I asked Pops/Frank about the issue and he was deeply touched that Whitney had brought it up. Here's our conversation, with Pops answering the question about where we each fit in.

Pops: My attitude has always been that every individual is an individual. They don't have to be famous or wealthy in order to be important. The person who does kind and generous things to their fellow human beings is just as important as a person who happens to be in the right place at the right time and becomes wealthy because of it.

Mitzi: Where does wealth fit into this?

Pops: Accumulation of money is not an indication of the more important things in life, which are one's relationship to other human beings.

Mitzi: What about a kid who isn't a success in school or doesn't go to a great college?

Pops: I didn't go to a prestigious college, and for that matter, I didn't finish college. My grades were only B- or C+ and I probably would not have been able to get into college except that it was easy to get in because there was a depression and many kids could not afford to go.

Mitzi: But maybe high grades are a predictor of how you'll do later in your career.

Pops: High grades in school aren't necessarily an indicator of greatness or a predictor of success. Wealth is quite often a result of a person, not necessarily a very smart person, being in the right place at the right time. In my case I was very lucky to have the right parents and had the good fortune to get in on the ground floor of a burgeoning industry.

Mitzi: Well, what about hard work?

Pops: Did I take fuller advantage of being part of a growing industry? Perhaps. Maybe. I worked harder to achieve than some of the others who had the same opportunity but that was partly because I was compensating for not being particularly smart. I felt I had to work harder.

Mitzi: Did you think you would be a success when you were Whitney's age?

Pops: No, I expected to be shoveling chicken manure the rest of my life. I had no dreams of grandeur. After two years of college, I knew that I wasn't suited to being a school teacher and I didn't know what to transfer to because I didn't know what I wanted to do. When I went home, I had no sense of ever becoming well-known.

Mitzi: The family lore says that you brought up your four children with the

idea that they didn't have to be the best there was, just the best they could be.

Pops: People need to follow their own star and be real individuals.

Mitzi: What other advice do have for those who come after you who find being in your shadow a daunting experience?

Pops: The important thing in life is happiness, not accumulation of wealth.

Love to all of you,

Sample Questions

- How do we deal with the pressure to be extraordinary if you have an extraordinary relative?
- Where does wealth fit into this?
- What about a kid who isn't a success in school or doesn't go to a great college?
- Where does hard work fit in?
- Did you expect to be a success when you were young?
- What other advice do have for those who come after you who find being in your shadow a daunting experience?
- Do you know what makes you happy?

Standing on Principle? Translation: "I'm Addicted to Being Right"

Notes on Using This Newsletter

ONE OF THE MORE POWERFUL CONVERSATIONS I CAN REMEMBER CAME AT THE Opal Financial Group's annual Family Office & Private Wealth Conference in Newport. I was talking with a businessman, Justin McEvily, about why businesses fail, and he said, "It's because so many people are addicted to being right." As we continued the conversation, he mentioned that it's often a choice between being right and having a relationship. The person who is addicted to being right never learned to put the good of the family above his or her own ego, and that person makes a terrible bargain by having the heroin of "being right," prevent what he or she probably wants most in life, and that is a loving supportive family.

This is another letter where it may be convenient for you to use a lot of the sample text as is. Frankly, I'd be flattered if you did! I give it to you! It's yours! But then again, if you have personal things you want to say on this subject, these are your newsletters, so please do what suits you best.

PERDUE FAMILY NEWSLETTER

Dearest Family and Family Friends:

"The happier the family, the healthier the company!"

This is a phrase we heard several times at the last stockholder meeting, and it matches perfectly something Frank/Pops said in one of our earliest family newsletters: "The most important thing we can do as a family, is to do those things that keep us together as a family." He understood that happy families mean healthy companies.

In view of the importance of this, I thought you might enjoy a conversation I had with Roy Williams, a family-business consultant with more than 50 years' experience. He and his team at the Williams Group have surveyed more than 3000 families on why business families flourish—or fail.

Love to all of you,

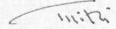

Interview with Roy Williams

Question: How often does it happen that business families fail to pass on an inheritance to the next generation?

Williams: We found that 70% of families wanting to transfer wealth from the family business to the next generation failed. In this case, "failed" means some combination of foolish expenditures, incompetence, family feuding, financial reverses, with the result that the wealth was involuntarily removed from the control of the beneficiary. Interestingly, this 70% failure rate holds true for virtually every country in the world. It even happens with people who win the lottery; 70% of the winners lose it all within a couple of years

Question: Why?

Williams: People guess that it's governance or trusts or other estate planning issues, but by themselves, even when done right, these don't protect a family from being one of the 70% that doesn't make it. I compare addressing only the legal and governance issues to putting a Band-Aid on someone who has cancer.

Unfortunately, if you ignore the core issues, those issues may kill the patient.

Question: So what are the core issues?

Williams: The biggest difference between success and failure is whether the families prepared the children and grandchildren for their futures. Does the family have a mission? A strategy to attain it? Is there enough trust among family members to carry out their mission?

Question: Explain trust. I think I know it when I see it, and I can recognize when it's not there, but just what is trust?

Williams: I'll explain by using an illustration of when trust had died, and how it was rebuilt. About three years ago, I asked a young woman whose family was one of my clients if she trusted her dad. "Of course not!" she answered with bitterness. "His priorities are money and business and I don't count!"

"Give me an example of why you feel that way," I asked.

"Last week he asked me to be at the office at 3:00 pm. When I got there, he kept me waiting for more than three hours. It was clear that I just didn't count."

"Did you tell your father how you felt?" I gently prodded.

"Yes over and over again," she said, and then added with a sad little sigh, "but he never listens."

Something had to be done and soon. I arranged for the father and daughter to meet at my office. I then asked the young woman to tell her father what she had previously told me.

What happened next was surprising.

She told her father how she felt about the episode, but even in this setting it was clear that the father wasn't listening. We asked her to repeat what she had just said, and even after the third time, I could tell the father wasn't processing the information. Finally, the fourth time, we had him repeat what his daughter had just said.

Even then, he didn't hear her!

It took three additional times of his repeating what his daughter had just said, and then suddenly, he got it. Tears started rolling down his cheeks as he blurted out, as if the words were torn from his heart, "I didn't know I was doing this. I promise I'll never do it again!"

"You will too," shot back his daughter. "I know your priorities!"

But interestingly, the breakthrough has now lasted three years. He had finally understood, and in the time since he has kept his promise, and he was able to act on it once he understood. His subsequent actions demonstrated that he really cared.

Question: You said you'd explain how the story would relate to trust.

Williams: Notice the four critical areas of trust that were initially violated and then put back in place:

1. Trust is made up first, of reliability: When someone promises to do something, do they do it? Initially, the father didn't keep his promise of meeting his daughter at 3:00 pm. It was part of a pattern of unreliability.

2. Second, is sincerity: Does the individual present an exterior that is not in sync with their true interior feelings? The father acted as if he wanted to see his daughter at 3:00 pm, but instead felt that whatever was going on in his business was more important.

3. Third is competence: Can the individual deliver on what's promised? The father could have been ready at the agreed-on time, but wasn't. But when we pointed out the problem, he was able to change.

4. Finally, does the person care? Initially, the father didn't care because he was totally oblivious to the fact that there was a problem. But once he got it, he cared deeply.

Question: So, trust was restored even when initially it looked impossible!

Williams: When you get at the core issues, such as trust and communication, and from there you get to the core values that hold a family together, and build on this to get to the family's purpose and mission, the results can be astonishing. I've seen this repeatedly: you have a compass to move forward into the future.

Sample Questions

- What's the relationship between the family doing well and the company doing well?
- What are the reasons most families are unable to pass the company and their wealth to the next generation?
- Do we need more than financial planning, and legal and governance help?
- What are the core issues our family needs to come to grips with?
- Are we preparing the next generation and the generation after them for their future?

- Does our family have a mission?
- Do we have a strategy to attain it?
- Do we have enough trust among ourselves to be able to carry out the mission?
- Do we automatically give family members the benefit of the doubt?
- Is there a family story of trust that was lost and then regained?
- Listening is a major part of making trust happen. If we don't hear the problems, we can't do anything about them. Do we all make a sufficient effort to listen?
- Are we reliable, as in, do we keep our word?
- Do we have sincerity? Does how we act on the outside match our interior feelings?
- Can we competently deliver what we've promised?
- Do we care?

A Cautionary Tale: Tear Your Hair Over This, or Better—Do Some Soul-Searching

Notes on Using This Newsletter

I'M IN FAVOR OF SENDING SEVERAL "CAUTIONARY TALE" NEWSLETTERS DURING THE year. My reason: among the biggest risks a family faces is family members not getting along. Anything you can do to guide their thinking towards remembering that they're part of something bigger than themselves is a plus, and it's also worthwhile for them to know that a quarrel gone bad can mean the risk of losing almost everything they hold dear. That's why I have included so many of this kind of newsletter in the Family Culture section. However, use them throughout the year as opposed to all at once. Have some lighter and more fun ones in between.

PERDUE FAMILY NEWSLETTER

Dearest Family and Family Friends

Frank/Pops often talked how his dearest wish is that the family grow in cohesiveness and harmony. He wanted that for you because he loved you and wanted what's best for you.

But there's an additional reason why it is good to think of the good of the whole family and never act selfishly. The families who don't, suffer terribly. I'm going to give you an example of a family that I was close to and adored.

It was a family with a patriarch and a matriarch, whom I'll call Barry and Alice Smith. Barry Smith, the patriarch, was a prince of a person. He was kind, wise, and as a businessman, brilliantly succeessful.

He owned many patents, including the patent for the process that makes powdered milk from dairy waste, and he also owned vast tracts of land in the midwest.

He had a loving wife, Alice, who was also a loving mother. The four sons, who were in their twenties and thirties when I knew them, were handsome, healthy, had attended the best colleges, and were fun to be with. They seemed to have everything going for them. Money flowed in, and to a friend of the family who loved each one them (that would be me) it looked as if they were the most fortunate of families.

But then something happend that under most circumstances wouldn't have had terrible consequences. Barry had a stroke. He wasn't gravely ill, but he was hospitalized for several weeks.

During this time, the brothers had what started out as a small disagreement on who would run things until their father's return. Tempers flared and the different family members started standing "on principal."

(As a quick side note, I have a lawyer friend who told me that he was doing mental cartwheels of joy whenever a client told him, "I'm standing on principal." For the lawyer, those magically delicious four words meant that the client had kissed rationality good-bye and would spend immense amounts of money to win. A client who stood on principal meant a guaranteed mink coat for my lawyer friend's wife.)

Anyway, back to the Smith family: Things escalated . . . and escalated . . . and escalated. By the time Barry was out of the hospital, the quarrel had became so severe that he was powerless to stop it.

Over the ensuing months, each of the four sons hired his own lawyer, and by now crucial decisions affecting the company and its employees could not be made. The family company was put in the hands of a court-appointed receiver who had the right to make decisions about this $350 million company.

Once the receiver was in charge, instead of running it, he sold the assets. The company was sold in a fire sale atmosphere at about 10% of what it was worth. Barry Smith felt that the receiver had only his own interest at heart and no interest in the good of the company.

By this time, the kids hated each other so much that they could no longer see that they were destroying themselves. They kept fighting until there was nothing left.

Barry had another stroke and died in the hospital, broken-hearted. Alice lost her grip on reality. However, while she still retained some of her faculties, she told me, "I tried to teach them everything and give them everything, but I forgot some- thing really essential, I forgot to teach them not to be selfish."

This story is sad, but not completely unusual. John Ward, the great fami- ly-business guru, can tell of many families that didn't survive because they didn't learn to put the good of the whole family above the good of the individual. In al- most every family, there are times when you have a choice of being right or having a relationship. Even if you are "right," does it matter if your intransigence cost you everything you hold dear?

There are some morals to this cautionary tale:

1. Don't let a quarrel escalate. No one wins, and the bigger the quarrel, the greater the loss.

2. In a family quarrel, do not "stand on principle." Standing on principle is another term for being addicted to being right. Which is another term for being self-centered. Which is actually another term for being stupid.

Love to all of you,

Sample Questions

- How important is family harmony?
- Do we do enough to encourage thinking of the good of the whole family?
- Do we do enough to discourage people from being selfish?
- What are some of the things that could happen in our family that could spark a major disagreement?
- Can we do anything to prepare for such an event?
- Talk about what "standing on principle" means to you. Is it an admirable trait, or is it irrational virtue-signaling and part of an addiction to being right that can leave misery and dissension in its wake?
- Does our family have an agreement never to bring in lawyers for a family quarrel? Do we recognize that when a family member begins litigation against the family, that there's an overwhelming likelihood that this means the death knell of the family?
- If we have a serious dispute, have we explored mediation? (See Mitzi Perdue's blog post on selecting a mediator: http://mitziperdue.com/family-quarrels-pull-back-brink/)
- Do we understand that there are times when we have a choice of being right or having a relationship? And that a self-centered approach to being right can cost not only the individual, but the family itself, almost everything we hold dear?

Importance of Spending Time Together: Making Deposits in the Bank of Family Closeness

Notes on Using This Newsletter

WHEN I'M GIVING TALKS TO FAMILY-BUSINESS AUDIENCES, PEOPLE OFTEN WANT TO know the secret of my two families and their ability to stay together for a combined period of more than two-and-a-quarter centuries. There are dozens of things that each family does to strengthen a culture of cohesiveness, but one that towers in importance is what I call, "Making deposits in the Bank of Family Closeness." And that means spending time together. For a nuclear family, that would mean having meals together and sharing stories. For families that include several generations and that are geographically separated, a valuable substitute is spending vacations or weekends together at least once a year.

Spending time together is an important concept. Use this newsletter to start people thinking about making time to be together. Feel free to quote any part of the sample text (here or anywhere else, that's what it's there for), or use the sample questions to spark your own ideas.

PERDUE FAMILY NEWSLETTER

Dearest Family and Family Friends:

Several years ago Frank and I attended a conference put on by John Ward, founder of the Family Business Consulting Group. The subject of the meeting was what factors create and encourage a strong family culture. Frank was deeply impressed by it, and one of the takeaways from it for him was, "Families that do the best over the long haul are those that have a strong culture."

Frank always recognized that families that have a strong culture and a strong sense of their values are the ones that last. During our 17-year marriage, I witnessed that Frank put enormous effort into insuring and strengthening our family culture. In fact, his willingness to take a day off to attend John Ward's conference was a proof of his interest in the topic.

He did many things to help support a strong family culture. One of these was to endow our family vacations, so they'd continue even after his passing.

Frank understood that a crucial element in keeping a family's culture strong and vibrant is the simple fact of spending time together. He understood that proximity, that is, being physically close to each other and spending time together is, to use a phrase he liked, "the sine qua non" (the essential condition) of developing closeness and understanding.

That's one of the reasons he took the somewhat unusual step of endowing the family vacations. We both knew from watching other families that after a patriarch passes on, often the family drifts apart, maybe seeing each other every few years when there's a wedding or a death. And then one day, what was once the family is no more.

However, Frank and I had talked about how the Henderson family has managed to stay close for more than a century. There are several mechanisms that made this happen, including a shared interest in philanthropy. Still, one of the easiest to replicate and one that guarantees that we see each other at least once a year, is that back in 1890, John Cleaves Symmes Henderson endowed the annual Henderson Family Dinner. It continues to this day, except now it's a three-day weekend instead of just a dinner.

I view the time families spend together as being deposits in the Bank of Family Closeness. A family that has a tradition of getting together even after the founder is long gone has a common bond of shared experiences and shared identity. I think Frank's willingness to endow the family vacations has been tremendously important for strengthening the family culture.

Spending time together is the lifeblood of family closeness. People who spend time together over the years own a treasure trove of memories that they can draw on when times get tough.

The family newsletters were yet another series of deposits in the Bank of Family Closeness. As Dr. Robyn Fivush, the Emory University specialist in families, says the families that spend time together and share their stories are the high-functioning families. They're the ones with a strong and vibrant culture. They're the ones that do best over the long haul.

Love to all of you,

Mitz

Sample Questions

- What helps keep our family together?
- What are some of the elements of our family culture?
- What are values that we cherish?
- How important is it for us to spend time together?
- What are the benefits of spending time together?
- What can we do to ensure that our family stays together in the future?
- Should the founder or current matriarch or patriarch make provision in their estate to fund family vacations or dinners in perpetuity?
- What are some of the holiday traditions that we need to pass on to future generations?
- How can we improve the family newsletters?

Families, Recipes, and Memories Thereof: Key Ingredients for Family Bonding

Notes on Using This Newsletter

FOOD IS ENDLESSLY IMPORTANT TO FAMILY COHESIVENESS. IT'S OVER DINNER THAT the family can reconnect emotionally and it's over dinner that kids get to learn the family stories and "what it means to be us."

But that's not the end of it. According to Joe Califano, head of the Columbia Center on Addiction and Substance Abuse, the number of meals you have together correlates directly with your kids' vulnerability to drugs. If you regularly have five meals together during the week, it's highly protective. The children are likely to have absorbed attitudes about who they are, and these attitudes help make them better able to resist peer pressures.

Preparing recipes from older family members is an excellent way of increasing the bonding that happens in high-functioning families. It gives younger members a sense of where they came from and that the world didn't just start with them.

Be sure to collect significant recipes because someday, Aunt Alice or Grandma won't be around to share those recipes with you. Ah, this makes me remember a recipe I wish I had asked for!

It has to do with boiled corned beef. Since my father was President and Chairman of the Sheraton Hotels, and since he recognized that having a great chef could make or break a hotel, he put significant effort into personally recruiting the Sheraton chefs.

One day in the late 1940s, father decided as part of his recruitment efforts that he'd invite one of the world-famous chefs he was courting to come for dinner at our family home in Lincoln, Massachusetts. But . . . he neglected to tell Mother that he was bringing home a VIP guest.

The menu that night was corn beef boiled with carrots and cabbage. Mother was embarrassed at having such plain fare for a world-famous chef, but gamely served the food to her five children, plus father and grandfather, and the celebrity chef.

The chef was delirious with praise, "Oh, Mrs. Henderson," he gushed, "I have never tasted such a delicious meal in my life!"

A moment later, father noticed that mother had left the table and seemingly fled into the kitchen.

Concerned and surprised, he followed her. Mother was in tears by the kitchen sink, dabbing her eyes with her apron.

"Molly," my concerned father asked, "what's wrong?"

"The chef was making fun of me," mother whimpered, burying her face against his chest.

"No, dear," father reassured her. "The chef was so used to fancy cooking that he didn't know how good simple foods, lovingly prepared, can be."

"Really?"

"Really!"

Mother looked happy again. She and father returned to the dinner table and she resumed being her charming and gracious self.

I remember the event because I was there, but in addition, it turned into a family story that I bet we heard a hundred times. But you know what? I sure wish I had the recipe so I could cook it while serving it to my grandchildren.

Recipes can be a magnificent way of connecting with your family history. Please, please collect the recipes while you can!

PERDUE FAMILY NEWSLETTER

Dearest Family and Family Friends:

I don't know how you got so lucky, but today you get to know Carlos's favorite Chinese dish. It's "Chicken Feet in Black Bean Sauce." I just know every one of you is going to rush right out and try it.

Especially Jan. But I think we can count on Sandy's loving the recipe also.

Okay, I'm joking. I really do have Carlos's chicken feet recipe, but I was warned that it was seriously poor salesmanship to put the recipe at the beginning of my collection of recipes.

You may wonder why I suddenly have all these recipes. Well, Rick Lloyd suggested putting out an e-mail call for recipes, and here are the first ones that came in.

The rules were, it did not have to be an actual recipe. It could be favorite take-out, favorite fast food, favorite meal to put together when you wanted something a cut above peanut butter sandwiches, and what to do if by some frightening circumstance, you ended up with a chicken whose brand name rhymes with "bison."

Enjoy the answers!

Love to all of you,

Lloyd Family Banana Smoothie

1 large banana
2 handfuls of ripe strawberries
4 heaping tablespoonfuls of applesauce
6–10 cubes of ice
Sprig of mint

Add ice and the applesauce first (applesauce provides the liquid necessary for the crushing of the ice). Crush the ice until substance is smoothie-like, and then add the other ingredients.

Anne Oliviero's Vegetable Melange

Cut equal size chunks or slices (about one-inch wide) of potatoes, green pepper, red pepper, yellow pepper, white onion, red onion, and Italian tomatoes.

Put in single layer in shallow baking dish, except tomatoes. Drizzle lightly with olive oil, add salt and pepper to taste (or skip salt). Bake at 375 degrees for an hour or until the potatoes are tender. Go by tenderness rather than time because ovens are often not exact. Halfway through, add the tomato chunks. You can also add zucchini chunks, if desired.

Clafoutis

(This recipe was collected by Mitzi during a family Nag's Head vacation roughly a decade ago. The recipe originally came from one of the G3s who is known to have studied at the Cordon Blu under Master Chef Don Enzo d'Oliviero. Frank loved this recipe so much that I ended up serving it countless times at Woodland Road. When you're looking for a healthy dessert that can be put together rapidly yet will still impress people, Chef d'Oliviero's recipe is a good one.)

1¼ cup milk
⅓ cup sugar
3 eggs
1 T vanilla
⅔ cup flour (if using blueberries, increase to 1¼ cup). Blend one minute in blender.

Pour a quarter inch of batter in a square Pyrex pan. Put in oven at 350 degrees until set. Add 3 cups fruit, such as peaches or blueberries. Cover with ⅓ cup sugar (or less). Cover with rest of batter.

Bake at 350 degrees for one hour.

Sample Questions

- What foods do you particularly remember eating as a child?
- What is your all-time favorite food?
- What is earliest memory of food?
- Do you have memories of foods you loved that were served during holidays?
- What do you remember from school lunches?
- Did you have a lunch box?
- Do you have favorite recipes that you'd like to share?
- What's the first thing you cooked?
- Who is the best cook in the family?
- Who taught you to cook?
- Were any of your children fussy eaters? If so, what did you do about it?
- Do you have a sweet tooth?
- There's a lot of talk these days about sugar being bad for us. Any thoughts on this?

Charitable Giving:
One of the Best Ways of Keeping Families Together

Notes on Using This Newsletter

OVER AND OVER AGAIN, I'VE SEEN THAT PHILANTHROPY IS THE GLUE THAT HELPS keep families together across the generations. It's certainly true in the Henderson and Perdue families, but it's almost always present in the cases of families that last for generations.

Philanthropy is great for the recipients, but it's a fabulous blessing for the givers. Families that engage in philanthropy have an inoculation against selfishness. Choosing to think of someone besides yourself guarantees that you're not focusing exclusively on yourself. And then I think of something from Frank's "Ethical Will," where he told his children and all those who came after him, "If you want to be happy, think of what you can do for someone else. If you want to be miserable, think what's owed to you."

In my opinion the biggest reason 70% of family businesses don't make it past the first generation is selfishness. People get into quarrels, they're addicted to being right, and they don't see themselves as being part of something bigger than themselves. These are all hallmarks of selfishness.

Being charitable may be the world's best inoculant against selfishness. Experiencing the joy of giving can be a barrier against the cramped, self-centered approach that leads to unhappiness. Use this newsletter as a way of supporting a culture of unselfishness.

PERDUE FAMILY NEWSLETTER

Dearest Family and Family Friends:

John Ward, a pioneering student of family businessses, says that a family-business's culture is both revealed by and formed by how it acts in a crisis. He gives the example of how, when there was a train wreck that involved IBM employees, Thomas Watson dropped everything and visited the injured in the hospital.

Perdue had an example of a crisis recently when a hurricane flooded the homes of close to 70 of the North Carolina Perdue associates. It was the worst flood that would be expected in that area in a 500-year period. How did Frank respond?

Jim told Frank about this on a Thursday evening while we were vacationing in Virginia. Frank dropped everything and focused full-time on arranging to have personal letters from him delivered to each of the flooded North Carolina associates, along with a personal check from Frank for $900 plus $100 in cash.

You might wonder why Frank didn't simply make one check for $1000. The answer is, the cash was to help the associates through the weekend. Frank knew that by the time we could get the checks to the individuals, the banks would be closed and wouldn't reopen until after the weekend.

Frank calculated that the flood victims would need cash for such things as food or, in many cases, milk for their children. I loved it that Frank wasn't only generous, he was thoughtful and able to intuit the individuals' practical needs.

There was a particularly revealing part to all of this. I was present when a man told Frank that if he'd only wait a week or so to make his financial gifts, his accountants could use the tax laws in such a way that to make his $70,000 in gifts tax-deductible. Frank answered, "The associates need the money now, not a week from now. Get it to them as soon as humanly possible."

I thought you might enjoy knowing more about Pops's views on charity, so here's an interview with him on charitable giving.

Love to all of you,

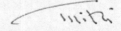

Pops on the Role of Charitable Giving

Question: What role do you see for charitable giving among your children and among future generations?

Pops: If you have the ability to contribute to those who need it, then you should. I would like to see family members contribute money when they are able, and even when they are not because they're not earning money on their own yet, I would like to see them contributing their time. I've enjoyed hearing about some of the community activities the grandchildren have been supporting with their time, such as Habitat for Humanity.

Question: I notice that a large percentage of your charitable donations has been for education, such for scholarships.

Pops: I like supporting education because it is such a direct investment in the person's future. Education helps a person be all they can be. It gives them opportunity. It gives them a better chance at a more successful life. The best charitable investment I can think of is investment in education.

Question: I've noticed that when you are giving a gift, you usually research the organization it's going to.

Pops: It's worth doing. Some charities that sound good put far too much of their resources into overhead and raising more money.

Question: Do you find charitable giving a satisfying thing to do?

Pops: It is personally satisfying. But more than that, it's simply the right thing to do when you are part of a community. My wish for future generations is that they be known as good citizens and contributing members of the community in which they live.

Sample Questions

- What role do you see for charitable giving among your children and among future generations?
- I notice that in your donations, you particularly focus on _____. Why is that?
- I've noticed that when you are giving a gift, you usually research the organization it's going to. Talk about this.
- Do you find charitable giving a satisfying thing to do?
- Do you volunteer for any organization?
- What do you see as a few of our community's needs?
- What charitable giving would help your employees?

How Can We Be the Best Stewards and Do the Most Good?

Notes on Using This Newsletter

THIS IS A COMPLICATED NEWSLETTER TO WRITE. IT ADDRESSES THE ISSUE OF WHAT to do when you receive more charitable requests than you can handle.

If your family business is high profile, then large numbers of charities are going to have you on their solicitation lists. The problem is that Bill Gates himself couldn't say yes to all of the people who would like assistance. The painful truth is that if you want to focus your charitable efforts, you will be forced to learn how to say "No."

So what do you do? Family members asked my opinion on this, and you'll find my answer in the following newsletter. You are welcome, of course, to use anything that I've written here (after all, I wrote it for you to use). Otherwise, maybe the sample questions I've listed can help you deal with the difficult and uncomfortable question of how to respond when you just can't say yes.

PERDUE FAMILY NEWSLETTER

Dearest Family and Family Friends:

One of the deepest values of this family is giving back.

As an example, my father, Ernest Henderson, told me, "The greatest pleasure I ever got through the money I made through Sheraton was in giving it away." And Frank Perdue was endlessly philanthropic in ways that most people would never know because often a condition of his gifts was that they never be publicized.

Still, anyone who comes from a family with resources is going to receive more charitable requests than they can accommodate. That means unfortunately, we have no choice but to learn to say "no" to some of them. I wish it were different, but learning to say "no" is a necessary skill.

This newsletter is a little different from most of the others because instead of my doing the interviewing, Whitney Van Der Hyde, as Vice Chair of the Education Committee, interviewed me.

Enjoy, and love to all of you,

Interview with Mitzi:

Question: You've had extensive experience with receiving requests for charitable donations. Where does the ability to say "no" come in?

Mitzi : Personally, I hate to say no.

Question: But you sometimes must say "no." When does that happen?

Mitzi: Well, as people who want to do good in this world, we need to focus on where we can do the most good. In almost every case I can think of, you can do the most good when it's a charity that you really care about. Do you care enough to want to volunteer for them, host events for them, show up at their fundraisers, or maybe serve on their boards? If a charity you're considering isn't close to your heart, then say no and instead concentrate your resources on the ones you love.

Question: So how do you go about saying "no" when you need to?

Mitzi: It's an art because you don't want hard feelings and you don't want the person soliciting you to feel bad.

Since I've gotten more than a thousand requests during the last decade, and since I found that I was repeatedly saying the same thing in my answers, I developed form letters to answer charities that I'll be turning down.

Although what follows is a form letter, it reflects my true feelings. And to repeat, I wouldn't use form letters if there weren't more requests than I can handle. Here's one of several that I use:

"I'm so sorry to have to be unavailable for helping with NAME OF CHARITY, but I've gotten too overcommitted in both time and money, and I'm concerned about not being able to meet my existing obligations. I worry that I'm not doing the job I should be doing for the organizations I've already committed to. I'm really sorry to have to say no, especially since I so much admire the _____ that you do."

Question: Did you ever feel pushed into supporting a cause that you didn't want to support?

Mitzi: At this moment, I can't think of a case. The fact is, I'm clear on what charities are very important to me, and I don't support charities that aren't important enough to me that I'd be willing to work for them. However, there are two exceptions. I will send a check if the amount is small or if my relationship with the person making the request is so important to me that if the requester cares about the cause, I'm going to care about the cause.

I try to resist persuasion techniques that would distract me from the charities I want to support.

Question: What are some persuasion techniques that you have come across that it would help us to be aware of?

Mitzi: Here are some:

- **The When You Want Money, Ask for Advice Technique:** A local charity asks if Mr. X can call on you to learn more about what the community needs. Your instinct is, "Wow, I'd love to help my community, and I'm feeling really flattered!" However, this is virtually always a preparation for asking you for money later. If you don't want to contribute to that charity, try an answer along the lines of, "I'd just love to visit with Mr. X and your project is so important, but I'm just not available now. I'm overcommitted." If you do visit with Mr. X, you'll feel obligated and you'll end up donating to a cause that's not where you may be able to do the most good

- **The Reciprocity Technique:** As an example, a woman invites you to a fabulous event, sponsored by the charity that has targeted you. This activates your "reciprocity" instincts. You'll feel like a jerk if you don't return the favor when asked later to donate. To avoid the obligations of the Reciprocity Technique, avoid accepting the favor in the first place. I don't accept favors from a charity unless I want to donate to that charity.

- **The Setting High Expectations Technique:** The charity asks you for a huge amount, to set your expectation of the range of giving to consider. I've heard that the Harvard Business School used to ask graduates for a quarter of a million-dollar pledge. The graduate may have thought of giving $5000 and instead gives $25,000. The best defense against the Setting High Expectations Technique is to know it exists.

- **The Social Proof Technique:** They tell you who else in your community has given large amounts. If the charity isn't close to your heart and that you wouldn't have otherwise supported, then simply recognize that the individual is using the well-worn Social Proof Technique Knowing about this technique is a defense against it.

- **The Guilt-Emotion-Reward Technique:** You see pictures that deeply engage your emotions, such as suffering children. (People studying persuasion techniques call these "pity pictures.") The pictures are engineered to play on your emotions, leading to guilt. The reward part is the pride you feel in feeling compassionate. People using this method may say, "If you don't give, we will have to close our doors and the children/animals/elderly will suffer." I don't know any defense against this technique, other than being aware of how common and deliberate it is.

By the way, I still hate to say no. And I love to focus on that far more agreeable and exciting part of philanthropy, which is the wonderful things we can do when we've said yes

Sample Questions

- Because we're a family with resources, we get a lot of requests for donations. Since there are more requests than there are resources, comment about why we sometimes, unfortunately, have to say "no"?
- What are your personal criteria for saying "no" to a charitable request? By the way, we all understand that we would much rather be saying "yes!" This is about how you choose to do this disagreeable thing, having to say "no" to what is probably a totally worthy charity.
- How do you go about saying "no" when you need to?
- Writing a turn-down letter is an art. You want to be kind, you want to be appreciative, you want to avoid being discouraging, but for whatever reason, you can't give them the positive answer they're looking for. Share with the rest of us some diplomatic ways of saying "no."
- Did you ever feel pushed into supporting a cause that you didn't really want to support?
- What are some common persuasion techniques that can distract us from supporting the causes where we can personally do the most good?

"Work hard, do your best always regardless of results, and if you've got it, it will show."

—Frank Perdue

Starting a Career?
Start Off on the Right Foot

Notes on Using ThisNewsletter

95% OF YOUNG ADULTS' FUTURE HAPPINESS IS GOING TO DEPEND ON TWO CHOICES that they'll be making: who to spend their lives with and how they'll earn their living. Helping the young people in the family make these choices wisely is all-important for the well-being of the family. It may be easy to leave this important topic to chance. But it's better to share your knowledge, wisdom, and guidance. In the sample text below, you'll see a newsletter with advice that Frank gave the young people in his life.

PERDUE FAMILY NEWSLETTER

Dearest Family and Family Friends:

One of my favorite experts on all aspects of family businesses is John Ward from the Family Business Consulting Group. He points out that according to Freud, the two most important sources of self-esteem and pleasure in life are love and work. He also says that in a family business, the two most important dimensions of our lives are connected, and failure or conflict in one will have an unfortunate impact on the other.

Today I interviewed your grandfather and asked his advice about how to choose a career. After all, it's one of the two most important decisions you'll make in your lifetime.

Love to all of you,

Career Choices: Interview with Frank

Question: Do you have any advice on career choices for the young people in the family?

Frank: I think that as far as choice of career goes, it is often largely luck and happenstance. I don't know of any formula except that it helps to have a strong leaning in some direction. Look for what you really enjoy doing whether in school or college.

Since being happy is more important than being wealthy, if you're doing something that makes you happy, that's probably a good choice. Also, it's surprising how often the things that make you happy can also make you successful.

I remember the case of my own father. When he was age 35, he took a risk by leaving what was regarded as one of the top-paying jobs in the county, working for the Railway Express. He did it to do something risky, but which he liked, and which helped him better himself. That's the way Perdue Farms got started.

Question: How do you feel about encouraging people to work in our family's business?

Frank: You know we have the rule that everyone can have a job in the company, but their advancement depends on merit, the same as if they were a nonfamily member. And another thing: I want everyone to understand that we're not running a country club. If someone doesn't perform, he or she doesn't get to keep their job. As you all know, I fired my brother-in-law and I fired my grandson. You can have a job, but it's up to you to keep it and to earn the promotions as a nonfamily member would.

Question: Why is it important to work outside the family business for three years?

Frank: It's an opportunity for the family member to stand on his or her own and learn what he or she is capable of. It's also great for the company, for us to learn how other companies do things. It's good for self-confidence because the individual knows that he or she is making it on their own.

Question: What should they look for in their first jobs?

Frank: When you're just starting out, don't be too influenced by the amount you can make. In your twenties, you learn; in your thirties, you earn. Your twenties are the time to find out what suits you and what you enjoy and what you're good at. In your twenties you have the latitude to experiment while later in life you'll have responsibilities that you don't have when you're young, such as coping with a mortgage or paying for your kid's braces.

Question: What about what courses to choose in college?

Frank: When I was in college, I chose the best professors rather than the most important subjects. You can get inspiration and ways of thinking that are much more important than the facts you'll learn in the course. The facts may not stick with you after you've finished the last exam, but the habits of mind that rub off on you can influence you for the rest of your life.

Sample Questions

- Do you have any advice on career choices for the young people in the family?
- How do you feel about encouraging people to work in our family's business?
- Any advice on how to choose your courses in college?
- Any advice on which jobs to take?
- Do you endorse the idea of deciding where to work according to where you can learn and where you can contribute?
- Why is it important to work outside the family business?
- How long should family members work outside the business? For three years?
- What should family members look for in their first jobs?
- What do you love to do?

Take Business Courses:
Be a Bigger Person, Contribute More

Notes on Using This Newsletter

SPENDING TIME, EFFORT, AND MONEY ON EDUCATION IS VIRTUALLY ALWAYS A WISE decision. Education can take you further along the road to being all that you can be. It makes you a bigger person and in the case of business courses, it will mean that you have more to contribute to the family business.

I also personally like business courses because in my own experience, courses in salesmanship, marketing, statistics, and accounting have proved just as useful to me in learning about how the world works and how people think as any of the liberal arts courses I took at Harvard.

Don't get me wrong: I loved my liberal arts courses and they enriched my life, but I am now a deep believer in the healing power of "and." It's not "either/or" it's "and."

This newsletter focuses on how family businesses can encourage family members to take business courses. As always, feel free to borrow any of the thoughts or words in the sample text, or pick and choose among the sample questions to help get you started.

PERDUE FAMILY NEWSLETTER

Dearest Family and Family Friends:

My father was always a big believer in education for his family. When my siblings and I were children, he used to sit us down in his library and devote an hour a week to discussions of morality or astronomy or how the banking system worked or what his parents and grandparents were like. Looking back on this, I treasure the fact that a busy, internationally-famous hotel-man took the educational part of parenting so seriously.

Today, I'm much older than father was when he was providing those Sunday afternoon family hours, but I still believe in trying to hand on knowledge. So today, I'm doing something I haven't done before. I'm interviewing myself about the importance of education!

Enjoy! Love to all of you,

Interview with Me On Education: Family Glue

Question: Frank always felt that education was important for knowing who we are and where we came from. But what about business education?

Mitzi: The more family members know about the business, the better stockholders they'll be, and thus, the stronger the family-business relationship will be.

Question: What about encouraging family members to take business courses in college?

Mitzi: It's worthwhile to encourage all our family members who will be attending college to take a basic course in accounting, in addition to whatever you are studying. The accounting courses have been among the most valuable courses I ever took, and that's because they are a powerful tool for understanding not just business, but the world.

Question: Why is accounting so valuable?

Mitzi: Accounting can be one of the best ways of getting a quick handle on what's going on in a company. It's like an X-ray in seeing through to the bones of the company. Numbers can provide this kind of insight. And one of the things I love about accounting is with numbers you can compare apples to oranges: just look at their price! As a writer, I tend to look at the world through words, but numbers, particularly in accounting, make me feel as if I've been granted a sixth sense.

Question: Besides accounting, what else would you recommend?

Mitzi: Without question, marketing. Marketing is at heart about learning to understand human nature. This is another priceless area of knowledge for a family business.

Question: What about business-related courses that you don't take in college?

Mitzi: I took the Dale Carnegie Salesmanship Course after college. The basis of this course is getting us to understand the other person. It's about persuasion and it's useful not just for salespeople; it's useful in life. I've sometimes thought the Dale Carnegie Course was as useful for understanding human nature and getting along in life as a couple of years in college. Oh, and it has the advantage of being a lot faster and a lot less expensive. Interestingly my father and Frank Perdue both took the Dale Carnegie Course and used to swear by it.

Question: What would you think of providing family recognition for anyone who takes a business-related course after college?

Mitzi: I love the idea! There are a number of business-related online courses that family members can take. If anyone takes a business course, whether at a community college or online, please let me know. I'll make sure that they get an amazing suitable-for-framing certificate from our very own (imaginary) Perdue University.

Question: Any final thoughts?

Mitzi: Education about business is important not just for those working in the business, but for stockholders as well. The stronger the family-business relationship, the better for keeping the family business in the family.

Love to all of you,

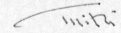

Sample Questions

- Should we encourage family members to take business courses in college?
- Do you recommend accounting?
- How about classes in communication? Or classes in speaking?
- What can we do to encourage lifelong learning?
- What additional courses would you recommend?
- What about business-related courses that you take after college?
- What's the role of nonbusiness-related learning?
- What publications or books do you recommend?
- Are there some YouTube channels you recommend?
- What about websites that you find particularly valuable?
- Are there any TED talks that are particularly helpful?
- What conventions or conferences do you recommend?
- What societies or associations should we consider?
- What about the role of joining country clubs or other associations for networking purposes?
- Is golf a good way to network?
- Have you used a business coach? If yes, has it helped?
- How do you feel about the slogan Frank Perdue used to use: "If you're not growing, you're dying"?
- What would you think of providing some kind of recognition for anyone who takes a business-related course after college? Maybe a special elaborate framed certificate or even a small ceremony at a family meeting?
- What about taking conflict-resolution courses?
- Can we have an incentive for family members who take the courses?

Future Entrepreneurs:
For the Business to Survive, Encourage Them!

Notes on Using This Newsletter

FAMILY BUSINESSES THAT LAST USUALLY NEED AN ENTREPRENEURIAL SPIRIT TO help the company stay abreast and renew itself in a changing environment. The book, *Entrepreneurs in Every Generation: How Successful Family Businesses Develop Their Next Leaders,* by Allan Cohen and Pramodita Sharma has tremendous insights on how to encourage entrepreneurism in the family business.[2]

One of the many insights in the book is that over time, the story of the entrepreneur who made the company grow is often airbrushed. I'm a passionate believer in the importance of stories, myths, parables and other ways of handing on the family culture, but there's a part here that requires special attention.

As Cohen and Sharma put it, "In generational family firms, the failures, trials, and tribulations of the founding or earlier generations often acquire a heroic coating as the stories get transmitted over time. The path to success is seldom straight, with many experiments, failure, explorations and small discoveries before success." Frank Perdue was a major success, but his story wasn't a straight line to success. I bet your founder also had trials and tribulations. How about telling your founder's story in a newsletter so other family members get a realistic picture of what it takes to accomplish big things? Use the sample questions as a jumping off point.

Knowing about obstacles your founder faced can help your family keep up the

---

22. Allan Cohen and Pramodita Sharma, *Entrepreneurs in Every Generation: How Successful Family Businesses Develop Their Leaders* (Oakland: Berrett-Koehler Publishers, Inc., 2016).

PERDUE FAMILY NEWSLETTER

Dearest Family and Family Friends:

According to Heidi Grant, writing in the May 2011 *Harvard Business School Review,* the most successful people aren't the optimists who are confident that they can conquer all obstacles.

Contrary to what many of us have been told since childhood, the power of positive thinking isn't all it's cracked up to be. Instead Grant says, "Believing that the road to success will be rocky leads to greater success because it forces you to take action. People who are confident that they will succeed, and equally confident that success won't come easily, put in more effort, plan how they'll deal with problems before they arise, and persist longer in the face of difficulty."

So take a look at some of the obstacles Frank Perdue faced and overcame.

The first obstacle, one that could have defeated many is that he started out as a painfully shy young man. He told me that when he first started, his father wanted him to get involved in the sales side of the business. The problem was Frank was so shy that instead of looking his prospect in the eye, all he could do was look down at his shoes and mumble his sales script.

And yet, Frank became a world-famous marketer. How did the shy man transform himself? He took the Dale Carnegie Course on How to Win Friends and Influence People, he made himself join social clubs where he'd have to interact with people, and when it came to advertising, he spent six weeks in New York City, going to the Association of National Advertisers and read every book, magazine, or journal on what motivates people and how to sell.

On top of that, he'd frequently call the authors of the books or articles. Some of these people were professors, but the farm boy from a small town forced himself to interact with them and become comfortable with them.

Frank's entire career was about transcending his limitations. I don't think anything dropped in his lap; instead, much of what he accomplished was the result of effort, study, refusal to be discouraged, and a lifelong habit of assessing obstacles to his goals and then figuring out a way to get around them.

I've just this minute been asking myself if I would describe Frank Perdue as optimistic. I don't think I would. I don't think being pessimistic or optimistic was part of the equation. I think instead that he figured out goals, calculated with utter brilliance how to reach those goals, and on the way to achieving the goals, figured out every aspect of what he would need to learn or do to achieve the goal. I guess you could call that optimism; he did have a sense that he could do it. But to me it looked more like almost miraculous realism as he went about the sometimes tedious, sometimes scary, and always challenging job of turning opportunities into realities.

Love to all of you,

Sample Questions

- What was the first obstacle the founder faced?
- What did he/she do to overcome it?
- What skills did he/she have to learn?
- Did he/she take courses or was he/she self-taught?
- How much was he/she an optimist?
- How much did he/she focus on the obstacles that would need to be overcome?

Do You Have a Plan? How to Stand Out: To Be a Winner, Act Like One!

Notes on Using This Newsletter

HIGH-FUNCTIONING FAMILIES SUPPORT EACH FAMILY MEMBER IN STRETCHING TO be all they can be. Frank Perdue used to encapsulate this approach when he'd tell his children, "You don't have to be the best, but you have to be the best you can be."

Not every family member can be a star, but there's a lot of satisfaction to stretching and trying to be the best you can be. Just planting the thought of being all you can be can influence the trajectory of a person's life.

In my own case, I started out by wanting to get by. But then one day I heard a speaker say, "Don't just get by. Don't just be a journeyman. Be a virtuoso." Those simple words made me raise my sights. They impacted my life. It was as if my mind was a computer program and those words rearranged the software so that I suddenly had higher goals. I'm not saying I've achieved my goals, but I know that I've gone way further than I would have without the higher goals. I've taken more courses, read more books, attended more conferences, had more coaching, and generally put more effort into my goals than I would have if I weren't aiming to be a virtuoso.

If you choose to send a newsletter about excelling in your career, please feel free to use any ideas or any words you'll find here, or pick and choose among the sample questions to get you started.

PERDUE FAMILY NEWSLETTER

Dearest Family and Family Friends:

A young man in a class I was addressing at a Columbia University business class asked me, "How do I stand out in my career?"

The advice I shared with him may be helpful to you also. I've spent most of my life observing who does and who doesn't do well in their careers. Here are some attitudes and actions that always seem to accompany the winners.

1. Go the Extra Mile

If you only do 90 percent of what they're asking of you, you won't stand out. You'll be average and there's no payoff for the effort you put into the job. However, doing more than what is expected is a great investment. It means you'll be the one management thinks of when there's an important assignment. You'll be the one with who gets the attention and the promotions.

2. Be a Team Player

I promise you, management notices selfish behavior, the kind where a person puts his own good ahead of the team.

3. Work On Your People Skills

Learn how to get along with others and how to bring out the best in others. Consider taking the Dale Carnegie Course on human relations skills. Frank Perdue took it, I took it, and my late father, co-founder of the Sheraton Hotels took it. And just how important is this skill? John D. Rockefeller said, "The ability to deal with people is as purchasable a commodity as sugar or coffee and I will pay more for that ability than for any other under the sun."

4. Learn New Skills

I agree with Scott Adams, creator of the comic strip *Dilbert*. "Develop a variety of skills that work well together. Each new skill you learn doubles your odds of success."

I've made it a rule always to take at least one new course a year, and amazingly, they all come in handy. I think it's a law of the universe that somehow, you'll find a use for the things you learn. In my case languages, database programming, public speaking, and even courses in design, have all helped advance my career.

The more skills you have, the more useful you are to yourself and to an organization, and being able to solve problems for an organization is an incredibly valuable career advantage.

So, to stand out in your career, go the extra mile, be a team player, work on your people skills, and constantly work to acquire new skills.

Love to all of you,

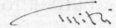

Sample Questions

- What are the advantages of "going the extra mile"?
- What are the advantages of being a team player?
- Why are people skills important?
- Why do you recommend continuously learning new skills?
- Do you have goals set for your career? If so, what are they? What is your timeline?
- Have you considered doing what Scott Adams recommends, developing a variety of skills that work well together?

Personal Security: Awareness Can Save You Fear, Pain, and Possibly Your Life

Notes on Using This Newsletter

IT'S HARD TO GET THE RIGHT BALANCE BETWEEN BEING TOO FEARFUL AND TOO carefree. I don't want anyone to be walking around afraid all the time.

On the other hand, I encourage everyone to listen to their "Spidey Sense" (the cartoon character Spiderman is supposed to have a highly-developed sense of when a situation is threatening.) If something tells you that a situation isn't right, pay attention to your instincts.

As Gavin de Becker says in his 2010 book, *The Gift of Fear* (which I highly recommend), victims of violent crimes usually feel a sense of fear before the violence took place.[3] Too often, they talked themselves out of taking action and suffered the consequences.

In his view, people need to pay more attention to their intuition. "Like every creature on earth, we have an extraordinary defense resource: We don't have the sharpest claws and strongest jaws—but we do have the biggest brains, and intuition is the most impressive process of these brains."

You might want to use this newsletter as is, or it can be a jumping off place for your own observations on personal safety. If you have personal knowledge of this subject, please use it and personalize your own newsletter.

---

3. Gavin de Becker, *The Gift of Fear* (New York: Dell Publishing, 1997).

PERDUE FAMILY NEWSLETTER

Dearest Family and Family Friends

The odds of your being personally harmed in an act of criminal violence are small. Most of us will go through our lives without ever encountering it.

And yet, the consequences of physical violence—lifetime emotional or physical scars or even death—are so great that being proactive in avoiding it is crucial.

It's no favor to anyone to keep them from recognizing that bad things can happen. In view of which, I highly recommend the book, *The Gift of Fear* by Gavin de Becker. He recommends that you listen to your "Spidey Sense," and if a situation doesn't feel safe, your intuition is likely to be right and you should take action.

He also says that people naturally have good instincts, and it's extremely common for crime victims after the fact to say they had a bad feeling about a situation. Looking back on the situation, they remember that something or someone didn't seem right, but to their undying regret, they ignored it. When you've got a bad feeling, pay attention to it and act on it. Move away. Call for help. Don't go there. And

don't let your feeling that you should be polite keep you from putting your safety first.

Here's some excellent advice from Perdue's former Director of Safety and Security and former FBI agent, Jim McCauley.

Love to all of you,

Mitzi Interview with Jim McCauley

Question: Are there any new types of crime that we may not have thought of when it comes to protecting ourselves?

McCauley: Something to look out for now is where you park your car when you go to a store or mall or social event. Stay away from open spots next to vans. Keep on driving until you're next to cars or other open spaces. What's becoming a common crime is that people will wait in the back seat of vans with sliding doors. As the victim, usually a woman, gets out of her car, the culprit will slide the van door open, grab the woman, putting his hand over her mouth so she can't scream, and drag her into the van. The woman has almost no room to maneuver or defend herself, while the culprit has all the room he needs to pull her in, and further, his van blocks the scene from view so he isn't easily seen by the public.

Question: What else?

McCauley: If you are in an isolated area and someone rear ends you at a stop light, do not get out. Don't inspect the damage or talk to the person until you drive to a lighted area where there are people. Ideally, you'd drive to a police station, but a gas station that's open is an acceptable choice. People intent on robbery, rape, and/or kidnapping have been using this technique of bumping your car and getting you to get out, where you're vulnerable.

Another thing to consider is, when you're driving, don't make eye contact with other drivers. Maybe the other driver is acting like a hyena, but just pay attention to what you're doing and keep on driving.

Another rule is, always drive with your doors locked. Don't have the windows open wide enough for someone to grab your hair or neck. The same goes for your sun roof.

Question: I agree about driving with the car doors locked. I was driving in a neighborhood that didn't feel quite right so I pressed the door lock button, and seconds later a horrible-looking man jumped from the curb over to my car and grabbed the door nearest me. Fortunately the door was locked! But what should a person do if a criminal has gained entrance to your car?

McCauley: If a person does jump into your vehicle and makes you believe he has a weapon and tells you to drive off or else he's going to hurt you, you've got to assume you're going to get hurt either way. If you're driving, speed up enough so that you'll hit something hard enough to disable the car, or go so fast that he can't interfere with you for fear of his own life, or go to someplace where there are people, slam the brakes unexpectedly, and dive out of the car.

Never go along freely. If they come in on the driver's side and force you over to the other side, fall outside of the car, get up, and run for all you're worth.

Your running and screaming will attract attention, and attracting attention is the last thing he wants. What he really wants is to have you under his control and helpless. If he does try to get you back in, scream, kick—do anything you can to avoid being taken back to the vehicle. Your chances of survival are a lot better out of the car than in it.

Question: What is the current thinking on resisting?

McCauley: If you're dealing with some-one mean enough to rape you or kidnap you, you are not dealing with someone who is going to keep his promises. My view is the only time not to resist is if you are unconscious. Fight until the end. A person on drugs may not be stopped even if you shoot them. A blow to the groin probably won't deflect them. But there's still something very effective that you can do in self-defense: if you stick your finger into the eye socket as if you're reaching for the back of his skull, he will be blinded.

Question: What if he's gone for your throat?

McCauley: That allows you to get your arms up and go for the eyes. If you have car keys or a ball point pen, ram it into his eye socket. That may sound extreme, but just think of what he wants to do to you. Or, if a person comes up behind you, slam the back of your head into his nose. Or,

reach backwards into the groin area and squeeze with all your might.

Question: What causes a person to be violent?

McCauley: The motive can be a power thing or a sexual thing where he can only get his jollies and turn on by seeing a woman terrified.

Question: What about swindles?

McCauley: If someone approaches you to invest in something with a 200% or better return on the original investment, that's almost certainly too good to be true. Get advice from someone knowledgeable and don't allow yourself to be rushed into a decision. Trying to rush you is a huge red flag.

Love to all of you,

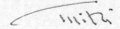

Sample Questions

- Any advice for us if we're in a parking lot?
- What if we're driving in an isolated area?
- What about making eye contact?
- How important is it to drive with your car door locked?
- What if a person has gained entrance into your car?
- If someone has gotten into the car, should we try to get out?
- What is the current thinking on resisting? I've heard people say, go along, and I've heard people say, fight for all you're worth.
- What if he's gone for your throat?
- What causes a person to be violent?
- Not all crimes are violent. What about swindles?
- How do you feel about responding when your intuition says, "This isn't right!"?

Cybersecurity: Information to Save Yourself Endless Grief

I'M ENDLESSLY AMAZED BY HOW SERIOUSLY SOME PEOPLE TAKE CYBERSECURITY and how casual others are. I know some people who install every security patch within moments of its being available (that would be me), and others who are—how to put this politely?—casual about it. I know a businessman, the cofounder of a major financial institution, who thought security patches weren't important and hadn't installed one in four years. He didn't think ransomware could happen to him and wasn't aware that he was putting his client's proprietary information at risk.

I can't know where you and your family members fit on the scale of how seriously you take cybersecurity. If family members are up-to-date and if they understand that being casual about cybersecurity can cost them untold frustration and expense, skip this newsletter! Otherwise, please use any of the information here or in the sample questions.

PERDUE FAMILY NEWSLETTER

Dearest Family and Family Friends:

Today's issue is cybersecurity. Fortunately, Donald Burns, genius cybersecurity expert for the company, is on top of these threats.

Burns has a fascinating background. When he was just short of nine-years old, his mother threatened to stop giving him wristwatches because he would regularly take them apart to see how they worked.

In his teens, Burns built computers, and later on in his career, he became a "white hat" hacker, paid to break into supposedly secure computer systems. His clients included the FBI, the Department of State, the Federal Court System, and the Department of Justice.

The company is so lucky to have him.

Love to all of you,

Interview with Donald Burns

Question: What do we have to worry about with cybersecurity?

Burns: Malware (that is, malicious software) can do such things as copy information from your computer to someone else who can then extract sensitive information such as banking information.

Question: What about ransomware?

Burns: Ransomware can encrypt all your files, including your backup files if they happen to be plugged into your computer. The only way to have access to your files again is to pay a ransom, typically in Bitcoin. The ransom will vary, but you could, as an individual victim, have to pay $500 or more to get a key that will decrypt your computer. And in some cases, the perpetrators are so nasty that even if you pay the money, you still can't access your data. They don't care.

Question: What should we do to protect ourselves?

Burns: The first and most essential step is, get an antivirus program.

Question: I'm using Trend Micro. Is that a good choice? Oh, and something else about Trend Micro, although I guess it would be the same thing for any good antivirus program: on a typical day, I notice that Trend Micro quarantines thirty or so malicious programs including today, five ransomware programs. There's bad stuff out there, and I could have been in a world of trouble if I didn't have Trend Micro and if I had opened some of the spam e-mail that I deleted without opening.

Burns: Trend Micro is a good choice, although personally I don't want to endorse one program over the others. However, I will tell you that for part of my career before coming to the company, I was a "white hat" professional hacker, and I was hired to break into companies' computer information to find out where their vulnerabilities are. Trend Micro was one of the most difficult programs to break through.

Question: What else should we do to protect ourselves besides installing a good antivirus program?

Burns: If you come across a USB drive and you don't know where it came from, don't put it in your computer; these unknown USBs can carry malicious payloads and you're in trouble when you insert it.

Question: What about a thumb drive from someone you know? If I give a thumb drive to dad's executive assistant, is she safe to open it?

Burns: It's generally OK to use a thumb drive from someone you know.

Question: What else should we have in mind about cybersecurity?

Burns: If you have any concerns that your computer has contracted a virus, it Is very important that you have it evaluated by a qualified computer technician as soon as you can.

Question: What about protecting the company?

Burns: We put technology that prevents malware from getting in. We monitor websites, email, and external USB drives to block malware. Ransomware is a particularly difficult problem because the people behind it deliberately target the people who most need their data. This includes the finance part of the company or the human resources people. In both cases (but there are certainly others as well) the people working in these departments need current information. The folks responsible for ransomware attacks look for relevant information on LinkedIn or Facebook on who works in these areas and then target them.

Question: How do you feel about using public hotspots, like on an Amtrak train or in Starbucks?

Burns: I'm going to sound extreme on this, but the cybersecurity risks you can come across in public hot spot can be extreme. There are more colorful ways of putting it (one of my colleagues says the risks are on the order of having intimate physical relations with everyone in the room and not wearing protection), but I'll just leave it at, "Don't do it." You may think you're not a target, but you may be more of a target than the big companies. The attacks are automated so they're combing through millions of accounts, and they're often directing their efforts at the easy-to-penetrate accounts of individuals and small companies because they're easier to get into.

Question: Why would the bad guys target me?

Burns: When they've hacked into you, possibly from a public hot spot, they'll extract your information and then sell it on the dark web along with thousands of others. There are organizations on the dark web where people bid on collections of stolen passwords and other identity information, and then bad guys with time on their hands will buy the information and use it for such things as draining your bank account or possibly turning your computer into a bot that sends out malware to everyone in your list. Or the malware can install a key logger which notices whenever you're inputting a password, and then they have a record of the keystrokes you use for not only passwords, but any security information you put in such as social security, mother's maiden name, and so on.

Question: What about opening attachments?

Burns: Never open an attachment without being certain that the person you think sent it is the person who did send it. If the person says something that a stranger wouldn't know, then I'd open it. But if the attachment says, "I thought you'd find this really interesting," I wouldn't open it, but instead I'd e-mail the person to ask if it truly is from them.

Question: How important is it to install the security updates?

Burns: Seventy percent of successful attacks come because you didn't act on the security updates. It's important to act on every security update immediately.

Question: Do I need to be concerned if my iPad or iPhone is stolen?

Burns: There's a serious risk that it will be delivered to bad guys who plug it into a machine that rapidly drains all the information from it. The whole process is automated: to get every bit of your information, they just plug it into the machine. They can steal all your information in minutes. Don't keep financial information, passwords, or social security numbers on iPads or iPhones unless you're certain there's no danger of the iPad or iPhone being lost or stolen.

Sample Questions

- What do we have to worry about personally with cybersecurity?
- What about ransomware? What should we do to protect ourselves?
- Can you recommend a good antivirus program?
- How important is it to install the security updates?
- What else should we do to protect ourselves besides installing a good antivirus program?
- What if a computer is slowing down or crashing or unexpectedly running out of hard drive space, or just plain acting not right?
- How do you feel about using public hotspots, like on an Amtrak train or in Starbucks?
- I don't think bad guys would target me. I'm not famous. Am I right not to worry about viruses affecting me personally?
- I've heard that opening attachments can spread viruses or other malware. What is your opinion on this?
- What kind of risk am I up against if my iPad or iPhone is stolen?
- Getting back to the company, what does the future hold for the company and cybersecurity?

Cults: They Target Wealthy People and Can Tear Families Apart for Generations

Notes on Using This Newsletter

AS WITH MOST THREATS, THE ODDS OF HAVING ONE OF YOUR FAMILY MEMBER succumb to a cult are slim. Still, the results can be devastating not only to the immediate family, but to future generations.

Something else: You may get the impression from the popular press that the only people who join cults are low-functioning people with few resources. In fact, cults often target people of means, and they particularly like high-functioning individuals who can contribute to the work of the cult. Don't assume because a family member is a college graduate and comes from a good family that he or she is immune.

In the case of cults, we know a lot about prevention; we know less about cures. The popular press may give the impression that interventions work, but in a great many cases, interventions fail utterly. When a cult has a family member in its clutches, it's possible for this to be a life sentence.

This newsletter is a little like buying fire insurance. You don't expect your house to burn down and you may never even meet someone whose house burned down. It still makes sense to fireproof your house.

PERDUE FAMILY NEWSLETTER

Dearest Family and Family Friends:

In the U.S., we don't know how many cult members there are, but the estimate are five million or more. That's a small number in a country of more than 300 million, but the trouble with cults is that the damage they do impacts so many others, as the cult does its devastating work of ripping apart families.

Anything that's a threat to a family can be particularly harmful to a business family. By the way, religion and altruistic movements are different from cults because their goal is to make the lives of their members better. They value and support the family unit and seek to strengthen family bonds.

Cults, in contrast, focus their energies inward, often towards providing money and power for the cult leader. It's typical of cults for the leaders to ask you to "prove" your loyalty by giving them ever larger amounts of money until they've got it all. Oh, and then they'll go after your children's money.

A destructive cult will use a powerful mixture of brainwashing, idealism, hope, and fear so that in the end, it will displace a person's former identity and replace it with a new one.

I've seen this in a family I was close to. I attended the same high school as a woman who became involved in a cult. Adele (not her real name) and I were close friends and I was fond of her. I still am.

In her mid-thirties, Adele succumbed to a cult that had clearly targeted her for her money. After a thorough brain-washing, she contentedly turned over her entire inheritance to support the cult. And if that weren't enough, she also turned over money that her children would have inherited.

Over the decades, I've observed with horrified fascination her relationship with her children. I once got up the courage to ask her, "Don't you listen to your children when they say, 'Don't do that!'?"

"Oh no," she answered. "I know how to defend myself against them. I don't listen to their words, but instead in my mind, I'm just saying my mantra. When they stop talking, and there's a pause, I just smile and say, 'Really?' and then they go on talking. But I haven't heard a word they said. I know how to thwart all the measures they take against me."

She was still a loveable individual, but when talking with her about her beliefs, I felt as if I was talking with a computer program as opposed to the interactive give-and-take that you expect in a normal conversation.

The money the cult took from her was in the tens of millions of dollars. She had been assured that for every dollar she gave away now, she and her children would be rewarded 1000 times over later. The cult leader assured her that God was going to reward her faith and sacrifice with unimaginable joy and riches. Adele believed she was making a beautiful investment on behalf of her family.

Her children didn't take it that way. They look at their wealthier cousins who can afford the best schools for their children, great dentistry, or enriching travel. The resentment the disinherited children feel towards their mother is endless and incurable. The cult promised this woman endless joy and fulfillment. Instead, it meant estrangement, resentment, and woe. It's sad.

Adele and I have stayed friends over a period of almost half a century. Her family and friends hoped she'd outgrow the cult, but she's been in it all this time. For a good bit of the time, her charm and intel-ligence led to her having a major role in the cult's recruitment efforts. People don't necessarily outgrow cults. It's perfectly possible that membership in a cult is a life sentence.

It's easy to assume that cult leaders target the uneducated and the mentally unstable. However, according to Dr. Kelton Rhoades, a man who studies cults, the ideal recruit for a malicious cult is someone smart, rich, attractive, and mentally together. That's their ideal target because that's the kind of person who can best further the work of the cult. With my friend Adele, they hit the jackpot.

What you're about to read comes from my beloved stepdaughter, Sandy Spedden. She gave me a pamphlet from the *Spiritual Counterfeits Project* newsletter. The original is available on the Internet, but here's a summary of some of their points:

Six Practical Steps To Keep Safe From Cults

1. Be careful about talking with strangers about your spiritual life. According to the Spiritual Counterfeits Project (SCP), "Many a young freshman has been sucked into authoritarian groups by opening up about the state of their spiritual life with some fresh-faced proselytizer. You should no more discuss your spiritual life with a stranger than you should discuss your bank balance or your sex life."

2. Be careful about "Bible Study" groups that are fronts for cults. Be suspicious if you are inundated with a lot of "sincere" interest and acceptance (it's called "love bombing").

3. Don't be taken in by the fact that they may appear nice. According to the SCP, "Nice people sometimes do terrible things. Often they are unwittingly part of an organization that is destructive as a whole. Civility and courtesy are not guarantees of truth, goodness, or spirituality."

4. Legitimate groups openly identify themselves. Cultic groups push for commitment before they disclose their program and practices.

5. Legitimate groups give room for questions and reflection. Authority cults tend to "railroad" people into their program.

6. Find out what kind of control characterizes the group. Do members have to seek permission from their leaders in making minor and personal decisions.

I sincerely hope that none of our family members ever succumb to a cult. Statistically, the odds are small that this could happen. But even a small amount of prevention can prevent a great deal of family pain.

Love to all of you,

Mitzi

Sample Questions

- Has anyone in our family ever been in a cult?
- Do you know anyone who's ever been in a cult?
- What's the difference between mainstream religion and a cult?
- How do cults get their claws into a person?
- What are some of the consequence if it happens?
- What can we do to prevent it?
- Is anyone in our family vulnerable?
- What can our family do to help someone who is vulnerable?
- Have we looked into resources or books?
- Have you read news stories about cults?
- What's really bad about cults?
- Is the family aware that wealthy, educated people are targets for cults?

"The most desirable trait for running the company is first personality, next drive, and last, IQ."

—Frank Perdue

Who Runs Our Company: The More We Know, the More We'll Appreciate What We Have

Notes on Using This Newsletter

THIS NEWSLETTER IS DESIGNED TO HELP CREATE BONDING BETWEEN PEOPLE WHO work for the company and the family members who aren't day-to-day insiders. In it, we'll be focusing on something of major importance in the life of the family company, and that is, "Who runs it?"

If there are family members who aren't working in your family business, then writing about the CEO (or another company official), can be a great way to keep them involved. The more people know what's going on in the business, the more shared knowledge there is, the more room there is for them to care about the company.

In addition, writing about a company official is a nice way to give that individual a public pat on the back. Showing public appreciation is a way to cement relationships.

What you're about to read is an actual newsletter I wrote for the Perdue family, and it was to celebrate a "lifer" at Perdue who became Chief Executive Officer. Most of this sample newsletter won't apply to your family's situation, but it can show you what a finished newsletter on this subject could look like.

PERDUE FAMILY NEWSLETTER

Dearest Family and Family Friends:

Today we have some important news in the life of the company. Randy Day is now President of Perdue Foods, and as Jim Perdue said in this morning's press release, "Randy has 35 years of experience at Perdue Farms, including more than two decades on the Perdue Foods side of the business, and fully understands our diverse and growing Foods business and the strategy for growth. Most importantly, he understands that we have a strong foundation in our values of quality, integrity, teamwork, and stewardship, and our vision to become the most trusted name in food and agricultural products."

What follows is an interview with Randy, reminding us of his history with Perdue and setting forth his ambitious goals for the future.

Love to all of you,

Interview with Randy Day

Question: What was your background before Perdue?

Day: I was born in Columbus, Ohio, but my family moved here when I was ten-years old. My father was a minister first in Salisbury and then in Easton. When I was twelve, I got my first job working for W.F. Allen, an agricultural company that grew strawberries, peaches, and apples.

Question: Was there ever a turning point in your career with Perdue?

Day: Yes, Jim Smallwood had once asked me, "What do you want to do?" I told him that as we grow, I see a need for someone to coordinate scheduling the plants company-wide. This eventually became what today we call Supply Planning. Several years later, Smallwood came to me saying, "Do you remember that conversation we had? On Monday, I want you to start that."

That spring and summer we started our international business and most importantly, the paw (chicken feet) business. Carlos Ayala (now VP for International), who was a student at Berkley at the time, was my summer intern.

We told people on the line to grade paws, but we needed something to grade against. It was easy to detect a broken or mangled cuticle layer, but with sizing, we needed a consistent reference for them to grade against. We tried to get sample paws to use for sizing by preserving them in formaldehyde or by dipping them in varnish. All of these attempts failed, but what finally did work was that we got an artist to carve a silhouette of the correct size on a piece of hard plastic-like material.

By the way, the late Connie Littleton didn't like that we were selling chicken feet with the Perdue name on the box. "Over my dead body are we calling them Perdue," she said, so initially we branded them Shenandoah. She was going to protect the brand no matter what. Eventually they did carry the Perdue name, but you have to respect her protective attitude.

By 1992, I was involved not only in production scheduling, but then R&D and quality assurance, and then logistics. In 1998, Bob Turley asked me to go to Food Service. "Bob, did I do something wrong?" I asked

him. Back then Food Service was not the big deal it has since become. However, Frank had foreseen that it was going to be important. I stayed there until 2008, when I moved to agribusiness, which I greatly enjoyed. Five years later Jim asked me to come back to the food side.

Question: Now that you're President, how do you feel about current initiatives such as Antibiotic Free (ABF), all veggie, and non-GMO-fed birds?

Day: I remember Frank was always asking us, "What are we going to do next?" And the interesting thing is that he wasn't hiring $10,000 a day consultants; he felt that nobody knows this business like we do so he'd go to us. Today we're getting back to that, doing new things. Things that we've been doing, such as ABF, have a shelf-life and competitors are going to copy us. We need to keep reinventing ourselves.

Question: Any final thoughts?

Day: I love what I do. I don't want to do anything else and that's a great feeling. For me, this job isn't work; after my family, it's my life.

Sample Questions for Company Official

- What was your background before working here?
- How did you end up working for our family business?
- Was there ever a turning point in your career?
- What are the company's current initiatives?
- What keeps you up at night?
- How do you feel about outside consultants?
- What's your biggest goal for the company right now?
- How do you feel about hiring from within?
- Do you intend to make the company more global?
- What do like about the company?
- Do you have any theories on how people should be treated?
- What's your management style?
- How do you feel about an open-door policy?
- What do you look for in hiring managers?
- What have you seen of the cultural factors that make us who we are?
- How do like living in our town?
- How many years did it take you from starting with the company to get to CEO?
- Was being CEO always your goal?
- Do you plan on staying with company until you retire?
- When do you plan to retire?
- Tell us about your family.

Innovation: It's Essential for Survival

Notes on Using This Newsletter

THIS NEWSLETTER IS ABOUT INNOVATION. FOR PERDUE, THE INNOVATION IS ABOUT growing organic chicken. And it's also about how we're doing more than just making sure the chickens are fed, sheltered, and healthy. We're learning about enriching the environment of the chickens and we're learning more about what chickens want as opposed to what we think they want.

Your family business is going to be wildly different from what I'm describing here. The sample text can show what a newsletter on innovation can look like. (Also I wanted to include this newsletter because I'm so proud of what we're doing in being organic and treating chickens better. I think this is the only time I'm going to sound like a commercial for Perdue, so please forgive me this once.)

Here's your chance for a newsletter on something that's of ultimate importance not only to the future of your family business, but also to your family's sense of what you're about and why you can be proud to be you. Choose some of the sample questions and interview someone in the company about what you're doing that puts you ahead of the competition!

PERDUE FAMILY NEWSLETTER

Dearest Family and Family Friends:

Because the family has asked for more Chicken 101 information, we're focusing in this issue of Perdues' News on one of the crown jewels of all Chickenlandia: our production and processing of organic chicken. We're the number one producer and processor of organic chicken in the US, and quite possibly, the world. As I said, this is a crown jewel!

Love to all of you,

Visit to John and Linda Brown's Farm

The Browns are the first to grow organic birds in Delaware. If you were to go inside one of their four chicken houses, you'd see a structure that was built in 1988, when they first started growing for Perdue.

However, there are modifications that make it very 2017. For example, the lighting is a mixture of LED ceiling lights and actual daylight. There are dozens of windows so the 16,000 birds get to experience actual daylight, and on top of that, to meet the requirements for being organic, the lighting is arranged so that the birds also get eight hours of darkness.

Something else that might strike you: there are various structures that you won't have seen in a chicken house before. We're experimenting with "enrichments" to find out what behaviors chickens choose to engage in.

You'd see a dozen or so boxes throughout the house, each in shape like a dresser drawer with an open top. These structures are called "bully boxes," and if a chicken should want to get away from other chickens, it can flop into a bully box.

Interestingly, you're more likely to see 15 or so chickens snuggling against the outside of the structure, as if they want to be closer to each other, as opposed to being away from each other. I don't think the box was designed for the snuggling together behavior, but the chickens choose what they want.

Another structure you can see throughout the house resembles a small lean-to shed. The structure is maybe five feet long, and the highest part of the incline might be two feet off the ground. Birds can walk up the structure and look out over the other chickens. They clearly like the bully box and the lean-to structure because at any one moment, you're likely to see all the structures in the house in use by one or more birds. I didn't count how many structures there are, but I'm guessing maybe 25. We've used time-lapse photography to see how much the structures are used, and they're almost always in use. The birds apparently love them.

I asked John Brown how much the birds use the outdoor pasture that's available to them. He says this varies, but maybe fifty "on a good day." I was surprised the birds didn't choose to use it more.

John and Linda are passionate about their organic approach. "We have grandkids who are going to reach the next century," says John. "What is it going to be like then if someone doesn't take a stand?" The Browns were selected to grow organic for the company because they have a track record of being outstanding and meticulous growers. They're committed to the concept of being organic and have been willing to do the vastly more extensive supervision and paperwork required for being organic.

Sample Questions

- What's the most innovative thing we're doing in the company?
- When did we start doing this?
- Was there initial resistance? What were the factors that made people hesitant about it?
- Who was the champion?
- Why is it important?
- What are the economic aspects of it?
- What is the impact on the people who work for the company?
- What is the impact on the community?
- Does it impact us competitively?
- Does it have any impact on how we see ourselves as a family and as a company?

Transportation:
Give It the Importance It Deserves

Notes on Using This Newsletter

THERE ARE ECONOMISTS WHO WILL TELL YOU THAT TRANSPORTATION IS THE MOST critical sector of the economy. It's also one of the most critical elements in most businesses. In fact, it's the lifeblood. If you can't get the materials, supplies, and people in and you can't get the products out, you've got a problem.

And yet for all its importance, transportation often doesn't get the attention and understanding it deserves. Today's newsletter is about remedying this. I think I can come close to guaranteeing that if you talk with whomever oversees transportation in your family business, you'll get a story your family will enjoy.

As with many of these newsletters, what you'll write will be completely different from the sample newsletter. Use this sample as a model and then pick and choose—or make up—the questions that will work for your family business, and then interview the person with the answers!

PERDUE FAMILY NEWSLETTER

Dearest Family and Family Friends:

As Mark Chambers, Senior Director of Rail Transportation, told me recently, "Transportation is the lifeblood of the company. You can't execute your commercial deals unless you have the transportation to do it." Frank put the same kind of attention into getting the transportation part of the company right as he did into growing chickens or building the chicken plants.

Recognizing the importance of transportation, I interviewed Rich Hernandez, Vice President of Transportation and Warehousing, and learned that Perdue Transportation, Inc. is so large that we're in the top 50 private fleets in the country.

Love to all of you,

[signature]

Interview With Rich Hernandez

Question: Give us a feel for the size of Perdue Transportation.

Hernandez: The Perdue fleet has 200 trucks, 800 refrigerated trailers, plus for the personnel part of it, we have 200 Perdue associate drivers and 200 drivers from other dedicated companies. However, that's 50% of what we do, and the other half of our transportation needs are met using common carriers.

Question: Why do we use other carriers instead of our own?

Hernandez: Often when it's a one-way trip, it's cheaper to pay a common carrier as opposed to using our own trucks for a round trip.

Question: I'm surprised that there are so many refrigerated trailers compared to the number of trucks.

Hernandez: Having 800 refrigerated trailers can help the plants with storage space when needed, and we have independent drivers, often mom-and-pop operations, who own their own truck or trucks, but they use our Perdue trailers. It works out well for them and for us.

Question: I've heard that your job involves a lot of math.

Hernandez: The core of our business is based on math. We're always using high-end algebra or occasionally, we even need differential equations. We're always balancing such cost factors as tolls, fuel, driver pay, maintenance, and this is all under the first requirement, which is on-time delivery and customer satisfaction.

Question: Give me an example of using math in actual practice.

Hernandez: I just had a meeting with drivers who wanted to increase the driving speed for our trucks from 62 mph to 65. It was something they would like, and at first glance, their request made a lot of sense: after all, there's a big advantage to saving time. I answered, "Let's look at the math. If you drive 650 miles in ten hours instead of 620 miles during that period, you've saved 30 minutes for the day."

However, for every mile per hour that one of our trucks is going faster, say from 62 mph to 63 mph, the fuel efficiency decreases by .1 mile per gallon. It's physics. More fuel is used to go faster and the engine isn't operating as efficiently. When you calculate that there are 200 drivers driving 20 million miles per year you get a cost increase of $80 thousand dollars.

That's when you only increase it by one mile per hour. It would be a much higher cost if the increase was three miles per hour and that's not even considering safety, insurance, maintenance and many other factors.

Question: OK, I'm impressed by the role math plays! What about safety?

Hernandez: The way I look at it is, "When is it acceptable for a plane to crash?" The answer is, "Never!" We're not authorized to fail, we have to deliver what the customer was promised when they were promised it. That means tremendous attention to maintenance, and it's also a factor in why we have a five-year replacement cycle for our trucks.

Question: What keeps you coming to work each day?

Hernandez: I enjoy the *esprit de corps* here. We're a company that everyone wants to be a part of. People have a passion for getting it right. We all know that at the end of the day, we know how we're measured: did the customer get what they wanted. There are no tie breakers: If something's not right, we must fix it now. We own it.

Sample Questions

- How important is transportation to our business?
- How important is on-time delivery?
- Who's in charge of transportation?
- How many people work in transportation?What's our primary mode of transportation? Trucks? Rail? Ship?
- How many pounds or items (or whatever the unit is) do we ship?
- Do you have any stories about why transportation proved to be important?
- Do we have driver training?
- Do we have an awards program for driving without an accident?
- Does math play a role in our transportation efforts?
- How do you feel about safety?
- How do you feel about equipment maintenance?
- What problems keep you awake at night?
- Will drones ever be a part of our transportation system?
- Do we put a lot of effort into having the trucks washed and looking good, since after all, they are a great big rolling billboard for our product?
- Do we have a replacement cycle for our delivery equipment? Describe, please.
- What's the best thing about working here?
- How are we doing in *esprit de corps*?

Employee Who's Been with the Company for a Long Time: Appreciation Is in Order

Notes on Using This Newsletter

I LOVE INTERVIEWING AND WRITING ABOUT PEOPLE WHO WORK FOR THE FAMILY business. This kind of information is important for learning what it means to be us! I think in my life I've interviewed more than 200 Perdue associates, mainly because I enjoy doing it so much.

However, don't worry, I'm not expecting you to interview hundreds of people. My grandfather was a historian so I think it's in my blood to want to record stories. Even so, I think that if you'll interview even one or two long-time employees, you'll uncover wonderful stories that make both the company culture and the family culture stronger and more resilient.

The sample newsletter that follows will be very different from what you write about a long-term employee in your company, but it can show you what a finished newsletter on this topic can look like. When writing your newsletter, look at the sample questions, and then choose and invent ones that work for your situation.

The person you write about is probably going to enjoy the recognition, and the rest of your readers will gain an increased understanding of what it means to be us.

PERDUE FAMILY NEWSLETTER

Dearest Family and Family Friends:

This issue celebrates an impressive milestone in the life of Perdue Farms. Elaine Barnes spent most of her career working for Frank Perdue, and much of this was during the period when he took the company from a small regional company to a world-class international company. This year she's celebrating her fiftieth anniversary with Perdue.

I've always had a huge soft spot in my heart for Elaine. It's twelve years after Frank's passing, but we still jokingly refer to each other as "co-wives."

Enjoy this trip down memory lane with Elaine.

Love to all of you,

Mitzi

Interview with Elaine Barnes

Mitzi: How did you begin your career with Perdue?

Barnes: In 1966, when I had just finished secretarial school and I was still living at home and wanted to work for a local company. At the time, Perdue was just one of the local chicken companies, but I applied and got a job in the secretarial pool at $1.65 an hour. This was 5¢ over the minimum wage and I was feeling good about it!

Mitzi: What was it like working for Frank in the early days?

Barnes: He was always terribly driven. I was OK with that, but there were his famous middle of the night phone calls to me and others, and these used to get to my husband. One time in the middle of the night, when Frank had something on his mind at 2:00 a.m., Steve grabbed the phone and told Frank in no uncertain terms, "Frank you don't pay her enough for this!"

Mitzi: Something else that he probably didn't pay you enough for, and something that, when I was working on his biography, *Tough Man, Tender Chicken*, I heard about repeatedly: the dreaded marketing reports. How did they impact you?

Barnes: There were ten marketing reps answering to Frank, and every evening they had to dictate their daily marketing report of that day's activities. We had four girls typing these marketing reports so Frank could get them the next day. After Kim Brittingham and I dated and copied Frank's handwritten notes, we might have as many as four stacks of paper, three feet high. Some of his notes had to go directly to the roughly one hundred quality control people located in each processing plant.

Mitzi: I can't even imagine the logistics of distributing all this material!

Barnes: We'd have envelopes for each person that we'd fill, making sure the right notes from Frank would go to the right person or persons. We'd have envelopes with everyone's name on it, and to sort them, we'd lay the envelopes on the hall corridor floor and they'd extend to the end of the corridor. It could take all day, starting at 4:00 a.m., to copy them, sort them, and make sure they went to the right people.

Mitzi: In my biography of Frank, I heard people say that they felt a lot of pressure to get back to Frank promptly when they'd get a note from him because if they didn't, they knew they'd be hearing from Elaine.

Barnes: It's true, we had a pending file, and if we didn't get an answer, we'd send a reminder.

Mitzi: What about his reputation as a tough man?

Barnes: He could be rough. He would get upset and lay people out and there would be bodies lying around on the floor, (not literally). Then when it was off his chest (he didn't carry a grudge), he'd say "OK, let's go get lunch."

Mitzi: Did you ever advise people on dealing with him?

Barnes: Yes, I'd tell them, if they didn't know something, to say, "I don't know, but I'll find out."

Mitzi: Since you've been with Perdue Farms for more than fifty years, what about retirement?

Barnes: I love yard work, but after a couple of days, I start thinking "I've got to be doing something!" Still, I don't want to be like the cartoon of the skeleton of someone who didn't want to retire still working at a computer.

Sample Questions

- How did you begin your career with the family's business?
- What's been your career trajectory? How did you start and where are you today?
- What was it like working here in the early days?
- How is it different today?
- In the early years, can you describe some of the management approaches that were common back then? Was it like *Mad Men*?
- Can you tell us about some of the things that were in your job description back then?
- What are some of the values that guided the company? Do they still?
- How do you feel about working for a family business as opposed to a publicly-owned one?
- Do you have a story about any of the family members?
- Since you've been with the company for so many years, what do you think about the prospect of retiring?
- Why did you stay all these years?
- What advice would you give to a new employee?
- Do you feel the business has a strong culture? (And by culture, I mean "this is the way we do things.")
- If you were Lord High Person in Charge of Everything, what would you change about the company?

Response to a Disaster: Few Things Reveal More about Who We Are

Notes on Using This Newsletter

CULTURES ARE REVEALED BY HOW WE REACT TO DISASTERS. FRANK WAS ALWAYS ready to drop everything to visit associates (that's Perdue-speak for employees) in the hospital, or quietly to provide money for flood victims or fire victims, or to phone people who were bereaved to condole them, even if it meant talking on the phone with them for an hour.

Jim carries this tradition on, and the family regularly skips giving each other gifts during the holidays, but instead uses the money we would have spent on each other to send hundreds of packages of gifts to overseas Perdue reservists or families who have experienced floods or fires. Families show who they are through their actions.

In your newsletter on responding to a disaster , your story will be different. Still, if your identity involves being a caring family, use a newsletter to tell about it.

One more thing: the subliminal (or maybe it's not very subliminal) message from this kind of newsletter is that your family isn't selfish and it takes pride in thinking of others and helping others. My mother used to say, "The givers of the world are happy. The exploiters of the world are miserable." Families that are givers are happier, better functioning families. Encourage it!

PERDUE FAMILY NEWSLETTER

Dearest Family and Family Friends;

One of the ways a family both reveals and strengthens its culture is how it responds to difficult situations. What you'll find in this issue is our response to a natural disaster in California. It reveals that we are a family and a company that really cares.

A few years ago, California experienced a drought-related fire catastrophe. The state had 12 major fires raging, mostly in the northern coastal ranges and the Sierra Nevada. More than 721 square miles burned, and 23,000 people were displaced.

I spoke by phone during the fire with Mike Leventini, Vice President and General Manager for West Coast and Organic Perdue Farms, and learned that one of the major fires was 100 miles from our facility, but even so, the fires were so extreme that the sun had a peculiar hazy color to it, and when you looked at the horizon, you knew something was terribly wrong.

 Six hundred homes were destroyed, and this fire was particularly devastating because it moved faster than even the computer models predicted.

Monday morning, it was clear to Mike and his team that the Red Cross would need food for emergency assistance to the many hundreds of people who had to evacuate their homes.

Leventini and his team sent 1,000 pounds of raw chicken to the Red Cross emergency kitchens, where volunteers cooked it and distributed it to the evacuees and firefighters. Mike was careful to give credit to his team since he was working hand-in-hand with them on a daily basis.

Leventini went on to say that another way we helped the Red Cross, in addition to food donations was that we used a mobile food truck designed to cook chicken.

The truck had been scheduled to go to one of our customers, but when Perdue associates explained that the food truck was needed for emergency assistance, the customer instantly agreed that going to evacuee centers was where the food truck needed to be.

Leventini was in touch with the Red Cross coordinator, letting him know we'd stay on, providing chicken as needed, not just during the crisis, but in the weeks that followed as well.

This was a big deal to the Red Cross because the need continues for many weeks, but typically, it's not likely to be on everyone's mind to continue helping once the disaster is no longer in the headlines.

Leventini was proud of the local support. He carefully noted that although we did our part, we were not the only ones and many other local companies and individuals did what they could as well.

Perdue has a tradition of helping when disaster strikes. It's who we are. Leventini and his team make us so proud. Thank you, Mike, Jake, Brian, and the whole team!

Love to all of you,

Mitch

Sample Questions

- How do we as a family and a family business respond when people in our communities need help?
- Do we give credit to the people who helped and made all of us proud? Is there a story, maybe even from a previous generation, of how we were there when the community needed us?
- What does it mean to us either to have now, or to develop in the future, a reputation for being there for our neighbors?
- Are we there for individual employees when they've had a fire, flood, or serious illness?

Environmental Sustainability: A Source of Family Pride

Notes on Using This Newsletter

THIS MAY OR MAY NOT BE A TOPIC THAT YOU CAN USE. HAS YOUR FAMILY BUSINESS been doing anything that's environmentally friendly or sustainable? If the answer is yes, this can be a great topic for you.

I know in my family it's a source of pride that we've won prizes for being environmentally responsible. In your family, if you can find things that the company is doing that can make members feel "we're on the side of the angels," it can be a tremendous force for family bonding, or as the Perdue family says, "family glue."

As human beings, we get our identity and our ability to make sense of the world from the stories we tell ourselves, and being a positive force for the environment is a great way to strengthen a positive identity.

Oh, and one more thing: if you can find the right person to interview (it might take a little digging), you may uncover sources of pride that you didn't even know about. In addition, providing recognition for a job well done helps with employee engagement.

Do you want employees to come to work excited to work there and fully engaged? Public recognition for a job well done goes a long way.

PERDUE FAMILY NEWSLETTER

Dearest Family and Family Friends:

Many of you know that we earned the LEED (Leadership in Energy and Environmental Design) Platinum Award. Some of you may know that out of 469 buildings in Maryland that are LEED certified, we are one of only nineteen that reached the Platinum level and one of only six classified as "New Construction." There's a big story behind these statistics, and Mark Beachboard is the one who can tell it.

Beachboard is the engineer in Perdue Purchasing who played the lead role in renovating the Perdue Headquarters. Interestingly, when Perdue was deciding on a renovation, Beachboard and his colleagues weren't even considering aiming for a Platinum Award.

"When we started this project," he told me recently, "we hoped we could make LEED silver. That was our goal, but as we started going along, we started to think that maybe LEED gold was in the realm of possibility. And as we got further along, and as we were analyzing what was possible, and what the costs and benefits would be, we realized that LEED Platinum was within reach."

The LEED certification is based on points that a building wins for being environmentally friendly. "We didn't focus on winning points," he says. "We went after investments that not only would be good for the environment, but that also made economic sense."

The extraordinarily good news for both Perdue and the environment is that there was close to a perfect match between what made sense economically for Perdue and what also benefitted the environment.

The most obvious example of this is the solar panel field that you can see as you drive by Perdue Headquarters. The solar panels alone, according to Beachboard, decreased our energy bills by roughly 40%.

The way the solar panels work is that they collect ultraviolet rays, convert their energy into direct current voltage, and then there's an energy control building that converts the direct current (DC) into alternating current (AC) energy. In addition, the low-voltage energy is converted to high-voltage energy, and Perdue HQ uses 100% of this high-voltage energy.

On weekends, the solar panel field produces more energy than the building uses, and the energy goes back to the utility, Washington Gas Energy Services. The utility meter that determines what we pay goes backwards when this happens.

"James Whitaker, our Director of Energy Sourcing, occasionally gets calls from people who complain, 'It's not working right!,'" says Beachboard. "However, the system almost certainly was working just right, but the monitoring system is so precise that it shows a decline in function from something as minor as a cloud that was drifting by."

Other visible environmental things that Perdue is doing include having an abundance of bicycle racks. Perhaps more impactful, we have a program in which associates who drive high-efficiency vehicles, such as the Ford Focus, or some of the Hondas and Volkswagens, get privileged parking.

We're also reducing the energy expenditure from lighting. "The desks are set up with occupancy sensors," explains Beachboard, "and if the area isn't occupied, the light turns off automatically. Further, instead of bright lights illuminating the whole room, there are individual LED task lights for each desk."

This isn't as visible, but according to Beachboard, we've benefitted the environment by massive recycling. "We've reused 95% of the existing structure, and we were able to divert 97% or 631 tons of construction waste from the landfill."

An example he gives is that when we pulled up the old carpet, the company we bought it from took the carpet back and re-used it. The same thing happened with the ceiling tiles.

We also used a third-party sorter from Dover. They went through the recycling dumpsters to sort the material for recycling.

Water reduction has been a major effort. Beachboard explained that you win a LEED point if you decrease water consumption by 10%. Ours dropped a whopping 42%.

We've done this by such techniques as using low-flow faucets and low-consumption toilets. Part of saving water on toilets involves a dual-flush mechanism, depending on how long someone is standing or sitting by the commode. If a person is there for less than a minute, the flush uses relatively little water, but if a person is there longer, the flush will use more water.

A major impact for our associates is improved indoor air quality. The air everyone is breathing throughout the day includes more fresh air coming into the building. However, as Beachboard explains, we practice energy recovery so, for example, in winter, when we're exhausting warm air, we recapture heat from the exhausted warm air and add it to the incoming cold air.

Beachboard is particularly proud of the company's air quality efforts. "Throughout the construction process we did air quality tests. We made sure that positive air pressure meant that we weren't bringing contaminants in from the construction."

They also chose low-emitting materials so items such as adhesives, paints, carpets, and composite woods wouldn't be polluting the air with that unhealthy "new car smell."

Summing it up, Beachboard says, "Overall, we are using 87% less energy than before, 40% less water, we've been diligent about construction-waste management, and we're careful to reuse existing materials and space."

He concludes by reminding us that this was done during some tough economic times. "We stayed the course and didn't deviate. A lot of people today appreciate the environment they have today. It's intangible, but there's benefit there that we wouldn't have seen otherwise. It says a lot about who we are as a company."

All those who worked with on this are making the rest of us proud.

Love to you all

Mitzi

Sample Questions

- Can you give us an overview of how we're doing on environmental sustainability?
- Do you see it as helping financially or being a burden?
- What do you plan to do in the near future?
- What's our long-term plan?
- What about cleaning chemicals?
- What's very specific to our industry when it comes to being environmentally friendly?
- Does the public understand what we're trying to do?
- Are we doing anything unusual or cutting edge?
- How did you get interested in sustainability?
- Are we, by any chance, trying for any awards, such as the LEED (Leadership

in Energy and Environmental Design) Awards?

- Could you assess for us how much of a match there is between what makes sense economically for the company and things we can do that benefit the environment?

- I know of some companies that give the best parking places to employees who drive high-efficiency vehicles, such as the Ford Focus, some of the Hondas and Volkswagens. Do we do anything like that? Are we considering anything like that?

- Are we doing anything to reduce energy expenditure from lighting, such as having occupancy sensors? Or LED task lights for each desk instead of lighting a whole room?

- What are we doing with recycling? Do we know how much money this is saving us, or how much stuff we're keeping from the landfill?

- Are we doing anything to reduce water consumption? Like maybe low-flow faucets or low-consumption toilets? If so, do we know what this has done for our water bills?

- What about indoor air quality?

- What do all these efforts mean to the people who work for the company? Does it impact morale, and maybe make people proud to work for a company like ours?

Wedding of Family-Business Employee:
We Cherish and Honor Company Employees

Notes on Using This Newsletter

ACCORDING TO JIM CLIFTON, GALLUP'S CHAIRMAN AND CEO, IT'S ENGAGED WORKERS who "come up with most of the innovative ideas, create most of a company's new customers, and have the most entrepreneurial energy." Further, on average they stay twice as long in their jobs, take ten times less sick leave, and according to Globoforce, the company that specializes in helping companies create engaged employees, the employees who are fully engaged in their work are 31% more productive than those who aren't.

So how do create more engaged workers? There's no magic bullet, but I can tell you what Hendersons and Perdues do. We act on the insight from a hundred years ago from the great psychiatrist Henry James: "The deepest principle in human nature is the craving to be appreciated." We lavish appreciation on people. We treat them as being as important as they are to us, which is pretty much infinitely important. That means attending their weddings, funerals, and generally showing that we care. And when there's a chance for public recognition, we go out of our way to do it.

Do you have employees who are like family? What about a newsletter when there's a major event in their lives?

PERDUE FAMILY NEWSLETTER

Dearest Family and Family Friends:

On June 20th, we had a wonderful event for someone who's been part of the Perdue Family: Cindy Downes became Mrs. Donnie Waters, and to my mind this counts as a Perdue Family event because she's worked with the Family and been interacting with almost everyone for twenty-four years. You probably have many reasons to contact her including that fact that somehow she is able to provide information that somehow only she knows.

This issue is about Cindy's amazing and wonderful wedding.

Love to all of you,

[signature]

Interview with the New Mrs. Cindy Waters

Questions: You've been widowed for seven years. How did you meet Donnie?

Cindy: We met years ago in elementary school and then last year we reconnected at a 70s-themed party. There was definitely a spark between us, even though all I did was hand him a napkin. He just smiled, and told me thank you, but the music was too loud to do much talking. Then about a month later, he was visiting his oldest friend, Brian, a guy who lives across the street from me. Brian, told Donnie, "You know Cindy's out in the yard working." "Yeah I need to go over and check on her," Donnie answered.

I was out weeding in the garden and he came and I invited him in. We sat on the front porch and talked for four and a half hours. I was just about falling in love by this time. At the end of this time, he left his number and said, "If you want to have dinner or something give me a call!" I made up my mind to wait a week.

On the sixth day he stopped. "Let's go for a ride," he said. It was around noon and we got home about 9:00 pm, and by now I am totally in love.

We were discovering that our religious views are the same, our political views are just about the same, plus he's a no-nonsense kind of person, strong-willed, and we agree on kids and family, which is important to me because I've always been a very family-oriented person.

Question: When did he propose?

Cindy: It was October 20th. On my birthday, he sent me flowers, and then over dinner, he asked me to be his life's partner and Mrs. Waters for the rest of his life. I said I would.

Question: What line of work is Donnie in?

Cindy: He is the Director of the Incubator without Walls Project and is the Business Consulting Coordinator for Maryland Capital Enterprises. He's a also a Perdue School Honors Graduate and has a Masters from Clemson University.

Question: Tell us about planning the wedding!

Cindy: We started out inviting 100 friends and relatives, but the number kept growing. We had only ordered 125 invitations, and after we used them up, we began inviting people by word-of-mouth. I mentioned to Stacey Desautels, the head of catering at the Civic Center, that I was worried that the numbers were getting out-of-hand. "Don't worry," Stacey told me, "you can be sure that 20% won't come."

However, 240 people came and Stacey told me that in 27 years, she never had a wedding that had 100% attendance the way ours did.

Question: What do you remember most from the wedding?

Cindy: It was at Emanuel Wesleyan Church, and it was an emotional event. I started crying in the middle of the ceremony and Donnie wiped away my tears. I also particularly remember the poem his uncle, James Tokley, wrote for our wedding. James is the poet Laureate of Tampa, Florida.

Question: And what do you remember most from the reception?

Cindy: It was so moving to enter the room and see how beautiful it was and also, having that many people want to share in this day made us feel very loved. Part of the reason the room looked so beautiful is that we were planning to rent things, but Jackie Cassidy donated an unbelievable amount, saying it was her wedding present.

I also particularly remember the first dance. Donnie and I chose "Share My Life." We didn't practice it ahead of time because we dance all the time to the radio so we didn't need to practice.

One more thing: It meant the world to me that Zé flew in from Texas for it.

Sample Questions

- How did you the two of you meet?
- Was it love at first sight or did it take a while?
- What about him/her made you fall in love?
- What's his/her most attractive personality trait?
- How do you feel about trust in a relationship?
- How long before the proposal?
- What was the proposal like?
- What line of work is your spouse in?
- What was planning the wedding like?
- What do you remember most about the wedding?
- Do you have a favorite moment in the ceremony itself?
- How are you doing with all the thank-you letters?
- Was there one (or more) presents that you found particularly moving?
- Did anyone give you advice that you particularly value?
- What do you remember most from the reception?
- What do you see for the future?
- Ask have you discussed money? (Financial incompatibility is right up there with infidelity as a cause of misery and divorce.)
- Do you share attitudes and spending and saving?
- Is one of you in debt?
- Has one of you started saving for retirement and the other doesn't care?

A Public Pat on the Back for a Family Member in the Business

Notes on Using This Newsletter

WHEN FRANK AND I MARRIED IN 1988, HE WORRIED ABOUT NEPOTISM AND HAD almost no interest in encouraging family members to work for the company. Jim Perdue was already employed in the business, and Frank assumed that having one family member in the business was enough.

However, shortly after 1988, Frank's attitude changed entirely. After talking with family business guru and theoretician John Ward, Frank learned that a typical family business needs to have four or five members of the next generation working in the family business if it's to make the transition to the next generation while staying in the family.

Based on this, Frank began encouraging family members to join the business, complete with internships and coaching. However, he did have the basic rule that they had to pull their weight and they would be held to at least the same standards as any other associate.

The following newsletter can be useful to you to encourage other family members to work for your company and/or to give a public pat on the back to those who are working for the company.

PERDUE FAMILY NEWSLETTER

Dearest Family and Family Friends,

This month's issue is on Chris Perdue, but the plan is for it to be the first in a series of newsletters, each focusing on one of the G4s (generation four) working in the company. My motive for starting with Chris is that he's just graduated from the Leadership Delaware program.

I thought you all might enjoy knowing about this because it's an honor for the family. One hundred fifty people applied for the program and only twenty-five were accepted. It was a year-long program in which members met with, and heard lectures from, Delaware officials in education, finance, the budget processes, research and development, agriculture, climate change, politicians, family-business owners, banking…you name it.

As part of the program, Chris has personally met with the governer and senators of Delaware, supreme court justices, CEOs of the biggest hospitals, officials from the Department of Transportation, people who make environmental regulations, and in the end, gained a whole year's worth of not only knowledge, but also networking.

Love to all of you,

Interview with Chris Perdue, Director of Inventory Management

Question: I know you're in Perdue Agri-Business these days. What are you working on?

Chris: We're always doing inventory management across our supply chain in the whole company, but right now we're developing and using ways of doing this at a level of granularity that we've never done before. In the past, we've been able to roll up the data into regions or individual facilities, but today, with recently available database and computer techniques, we can get data right down to a single truckload or farm

Question: And the difference this degree of drilling down makes to the company?

Chris: We're finding small opportunities which, when you add them together, can mean many millions of dollars in savings. For example, every time a truck goes out empty and comes back full, we've lost 50% of the truck's potential earning capacity. We could save millions of dollars on trucks and trains by optimizing routes. .

Another example is the cost analysis of processing the different grains. We know that in a particular grain elevator, it can cost 25 cents to run a bushel of grain, but the cost for processing corn varies in different facilities from the cost of processing soybeans or wheat. With more precise figures, we know where to direct grain shipments. The information lets us know where we should handle which grains and how to move them.

Question: What got you interested?

Chris: I have a biology background, but I've always had a personal passion for programming and computer science. My biology degree set me up for the critical analysis of data, and I've been creating forecasting algorithms and geospatial models in recent years. I can write algorithms, put them in an Excel pivot table, and the results are new, with extraordinarily more accessible and actionable information.

Question: How did you go about developing the information behind the algorithms?

Chris: I spent ten weeks in my truck visiting all our seventy-five agri-business locations. I toured every facility, got to know how every operation functions and how it's part of the larger picture. In some cases, the facilities are so small that it's only two guys in a grain elevator. I traveled 8,500 miles to do this. It allowed me to know what data points I should be hunting for when I build the predictive models.

Question: What about the future?

Chris: We need to hire young people with data management forecasting skills, and we need to pair them with statisticians and economists. The big savings and big improvements are going to come as we create business intelligence that enables new ways of looking at things. It's this kind of information that allows every associate to find all the answers he or she needs. Having real-world, accurate information equips them to unlock their full potential.

Sample Questions

- How well is our family doing in keeping up with the family members who are working in the business? Should we do more?
- Have any of our family members won an award related to their work?
- Have any had a promotion?
- Is an honor for one of us an honor for all?
- What department are you in and how long have you been working there?
- What does your department do? What issues is your department facing?
- What are you focusing on now?
- Are there any opportunities that excite you?
- How did you happen to get interested in this?
- Is there a technological aspect for this?
- Is there an international aspect for this?
- Is there a sustainability aspect for this?
- Is there a competitive advantage to it?
- How is the industry doing relative to us?
- Do you interact a lot with the employees? Are there big savings and improvements that you can foresee?

Recognition: It Demonstrates and Reinforces What We Value

Notes on Using This Newsletter

RECOGNITION IS ONE OF THE WAYS A CULTURE GETS EMBEDDED. RECOGNITION IS A "positional good," signaling the receiver's relative standing in society. People seek recognition and feel rewarded by it in ways that are surprisingly similar to how they respond to money.

Given it's emotional and motivational impact, it's worth paying attention to what actions or attitudes get rewarded with recognition. This newsletter talks about how Perdue Farms uses recognition.

Your family business will be different, but if you'll use the sample text as an example of what a finished letter might look like, and then use the sample questions later on as a jumping-off place for your newsletter, you'll be doing something important for further embedding the culture that makes your family business what it is.

PERDUE FAMILY NEWSLETTER

Dearest Family and Family Friends:

One of the most impactful ways of embedding a positive culture in the family business is how we allocate awards. I was always surprised at how acutely Frank was aware of this.

In fact I've often wondered where he got this understanding, coming as he did from a small town and growing up an only child. As a boy, instead of socializing with his classmates, he was known for spending almost all his available time helping his dad on the farm.

And yet, this shy, isolated young person somehow developed an almost preternatural understanding of human nature. Who would have predicted that a shy and lonely boy could have developed a world-class awareness of what makes us human beings tick?

I suppose one of the things that may have helped is he was a tremendous reader. He once told me that by age twelve he had read every book in his school's library. To the end of his days, he was reading books on every possible subject, from a biogra-phy of Elizabeth the Great of Russia to the latest John Grisham novel.

Maybe his understanding of human nature was helped along by his having been such a reader. He understood what the great psychologist William James said more than a century ago: "The deepest principle in human nature is the craving to be appreciated."

Anyway, with his acute sense of how important recognition is, Frank put enormous effort into every conceivable aspect of it.

He was hugely involved in the criteria for recognition. As an example, plant safety was of preeminent importance to him. He therefore made it a point to attend every plant's safety celebrations. When a plant or when truck drivers had achieved either a million man-hours or a million miles without an accident, they could count on his being there to emphasize the importance of the event.

He'd do this even if it meant getting up at 2:00 am and driving two hours to attend the celebration for a night shift's safety awards.

He and I also regularly attended graduation ceremonies for employees who had attended "English as a Second Language" classes. He did this because he wanted to make sure that people from other countries had a chance at supervisory positions. Showing appreciation for individuals who graduated from these courses was something that Frank would do as a matter of course. Frank put a fabulous amount of effort into showing people that they were important and that he cared. It was one of his secrets of success. His awarding of appreciation and recognition helped make for a strong culture. It was one of the reasons that people who lasted for five years at Perdue usually stayed with him for life.

Love to all of you,

Sample Questions

- How do we as a family business use recognition as a way of embedding the company values?
- How do we increase our understanding of human motivation?
- What positive aspects of the company culture do we reinforce by awards or recognition?
- Do our criteria for awarding status and recognition contribute to employee retention?
- What are some of the values we reward?
- What prizes do we award?
- What ways do we show recognition? Parties? Service awards? Prizes? Employee-of-the-month ceremonies?
- Are there some ways of using recognition that we should be using, but haven't yet?
- Has paying attention to recognition and the criteria for recognition been beneficial for us?

Prenuptial Agreements: An Insurance Policy for All the Company's Stakeholders

Notes on Using This Newsletter

PRENUPTIAL AGREEMENTS ARE A SERIOUSLY UNCOMFORTABLE TOPIC. BUT STILL, it's worth dealing with the topic way ahead of time. Too many companies have been gravely harmed or destroyed through divorce, and that means collateral damage to employees, stockholders, the communities, the lenders, and innocent bystanders.

Keep in mind that the prenuptial agreement isn't about the couple in question; it's an insurance policy on behalf of all the other stakeholders who would be impacted by a difficult divorce.

In the case of this newsletter, it may be easiest to copy large parts of the sample newsletter. That's what it's there for. But equally good (if not equally easy), put everything in your own words, and I hope the sample questions will help you get started.

PERDUE FAMILY NEWSLETTER

Dearest Family and Family Friends:

You can find issues more uncomfortable than prenuptial agreements. But not many.

For starters, people view prenups from amazingly different points of view. One of my granddaughter's professors told her that asking anyone for a prenup was so demeaning and exploitive that even asking for one would be grounds for breaking an engagement.

On the other side, a social friend of mine has the attitude, "Anyone who won't sign a prenup, is after your money." She told her son that if a woman was unwilling to sign a prenup, that would be disqualifying. "Why should she be paid for marrying you?" the mother asked.

My own view is somewhere in the middle, but I do believe that for members of a family business, marriage isn't about just two individuals. A divorce could impact the family, the employees, the lenders, the customers, and the community.

Love to all of you,

Interview with Pops

Question: Why should family members consider a prenuptial agreement?

Pops: I know of too many cases where a divorce damaged or destroyed an on-going business. The collateral damage from a bankruptcy or hostile takeover or brand damage can be disastrous for countless innocent bystanders.

I heard of a traumatic story recently. There's a company that has been in business for more than ninety years, but it's survival is in doubt today. Up until recently, the business was a success, but the two sons are each going through painful divorces. They didn't have pre-nuptial agreements and their spouses are now claiming half of their shares in the company. This is terrible for the company because the ex-wives aren't interested in the company's long-term success and instead want to get as much money out of it as possible right now. A lot of grief and sleepless nights would have been avoided if the two young men had had prenuptial agreements.

Question: Talk more about the consequences of not having a prenup.

Pops: For business-owning families, the essential purpose of premarital agreements is to help keep the family business in the family for the sake of future generations. Without premarital agreements, shares in the business could be taken away through divorce proceedings. Your children and grandchildren may not have a company to be a part of.

Question: But a prenup isn't romantic!

Pops: It's not romantic and the discussions that go into it are not comfortable. However, that won't be the only time in your life that you and your intended are going to have difficult discussions and this can give you important insight into how you both are able to deal with difficult discussions during your marriage. You have the choice of sweeping this conversation under the rug or facing it openly. You're vastly better off dealing with it openly and honestly.

Question: But why not sweep it under the rug? Let's suppose the young couple loves and trusts each other. Why isn't this just between the two of them?

Pops: A marriage isn't only a romantic and an intimate relationship. It's about families, inheritance, an on-going business, and without a prenup that protects the business, a family member could be putting others at risk.

Question: So how does a young person who's in love bring it up? Or maybe I'll answer that one myself. I'd say explain to your intended this is not personal, but this is how the family he or she is marrying into does things. Marriage-age family members need to understand that the prenuptial agreement is part of the family's risk-management plan, it isn't personally directed at anyone. It's an insurance policy taken out on behalf of all the company's stakeholders.

Question: When should a family member bring up the subject of a prenup?

Pops: The earlier the better, for instance when you're first starting to think about spending your lives together.

Sample Questions

- Why should family members consider a prenuptial agreement?
- Can you talk more about the consequences of not having a prenup?
- How do you deal with the fact that a prenup isn't romantic?
- Why not sweep it under the rug? We love each other and we trust each other! Why isn't this just between us?
- So how do I bring it up?
- When should I bring it up?
- Is it important to redo the document as conditions change?
- What are some of the provisions that should be included for a spouse who substantially contributes to the business.
- How much will you value the contributions of the nonworking spouse?
- How much value do you put on a stable home life if the spouse doesn't work?

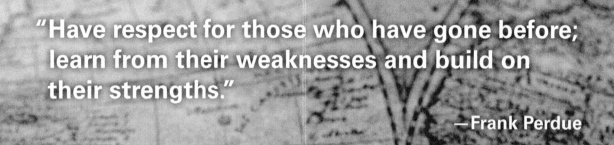

"Have respect for those who have gone before;
learn from their weaknesses and build on
their strengths."

—Frank Perdue

Our Founder Was a Real Person Who Struggled before He Succeeded

Notes on Using This Newsletter

I'M A HUGE FAN OF DR. ROBYN FIVUSH AND HER STUDIES AT EMORY UNIVERSITY on high-functioning families. Her research shows that the healthiest and most successful families have a strong identity and a strong culture. They know their family stories and values, and they know the "why" as well as the "what" that makes their families tick.

This newsletter introduces family members to some of the values that Frank Perdue wanted to transmit to his descendants. Your version of this newsletter will almost certainly be different, but this can serve as a model for how to present the subject.

PERDUE FAMILY NEWSLETTER

Dearest Family and Family Friends:

I hope you'll enjoy knowing the stories about your family. As you read this and future issues about people who have played major roles in our family business, you'll have a better understanding of where you came from, and what values your family had and what they hoped for your future.

Love,

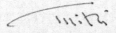

Sample Interview with Pops (who is really Frank Perdue)

Question: What values do you hope to pass on to those who come after you?

Pops: I hope they'll instill in their own children and grandchildren a notion of stewardship. Being a good steward includes many things, but an important part is aiming to hand your inheritance on intact to the next generation.

Question: Do you have any suggestions for achieving this?

Pops: Yes, and the first is, it's okay to spend the income from your inheritance, but please, never invade the principal. By law, your inheritance is yours and you can do anything you want with it. Still it is my hope that you'll treat it, not as your own, but as something that you've borrowed from your children.

Question: Any other suggestions?

Pops: The second suggestion, and it's a somewhat painful one, is be aware that you are an obvious target for people who want to separate you from your wealth.

For many of you, this is not something that you need to worry about right now. But, when you are older, you will find many times that people will come to you with "can't lose" investment opportunities.

The investment will sound wonderful— because it's meant to! It wouldn't be a danger if it didn't sound so absolutely great.

However, I can tell you that I have seen many people who have inherited wealth lose it all to unsafe investments.

When someone comes to you with a get-rich-quick scheme, and wants you to invest in it, have an older and wiser person give you an opinion on it. By the time a family member is an adult, he or she should have an investment advisor.

Question: Besides get-rich-quick schemes, are there other telltale signs that we should be on the lookout for, when someone is tempting us with an investment that might not be a good idea?

Pops: One of the hallmarks of someone who's making an unscrupulous offer is that they'll try to put you under a severe time pressure. The offer would be couched in terms like, "There are three people who want this and I don't think it's going to be available even twenty-four hours from now!"

The reason for the rush is, they don't want you to think about it calmly and they don't want you to consult others about this "once-in-a-lifetime opportunity."

When someone puts pressure on you to act quickly, it's possible that it's legitimate. But more often, it's a tactic of the unscrupulous.

Sample Questions

- What values do you hope to pass on to those who come after you?
- In our family, whom should younger members go to for advice we can trust?
- What telltale signs should we be on the lookout for, when someone is tempting us with a get-rich-quick scheme?
- What challenges did you face?
- Why did you start the business?
- What do you wish you had done differently?
- What worked really well?
- What vision do you have for the future?
- Do you want us to stay a private company?
- What are the advantage of working for the company instead of going out and working someplace else.
- What education do you wish you had?

Reminiscences from an Older Family Member:
A History with Fascinating Stories

Notes on Using This Newsletter

YOUR NEWSLETTER, BECAUSE IT'S ABOUT YOUR FAMILY MEMBER, WILL BE ENTIRELY different from the sample newsletter. The purpose here is to show how it might look, but the content will be different.

I bet as you start asking your older family member questions about long ago, you'll come up with surprising, entertaining, and fun stories about his or her life. Even better, the family members who read what you write are going to know more about their roots and more about who they are.

It will deepen their sense of "who we are" and "where we came from." In short, this kind of information strengthens the family culture.

I think you'll enjoy the process of interviewing an older family member.

PERDUE FAMILY NEWSLETTER

Dearest Family Members:

This month's issue of our family's newsletter is about "where we came from."

I interviewed Grandma Alice about what it was like growing up, and I hope you'll find it as interesting as I did.

Love to all of you,

Interview with Grandma Alice Turner

Question: When and where were you born?

Grandma: I was born on May 3rd, 1920, in Wheeling, West Virginia.

Question: Did you have brothers and sisters? How many?

Grandma: There were eight children in my family, and this was an average size farm family. You needed a large family to run the farm and every child had a job to do from the time they were five years old. Question: Did you have chores?

Grandma: Before I went to school, I had to get up in the morning, put on my old work clothes and bring in the firewood for heating the house and for cooking. I also had to carry water for the pigs because there wasn't any running water in our piggery.

Question: What was something different back then, something that would surprise people today?

Grandma: One of the things that would be hard for young people today to imagine was what it was like before houses had modern insulation. The walls hardly slowed down the wind. The only heat in the house came from the wood-burning stove in the kitchen. Our bedrooms were as cold inside as it was outdoors. When it was cold, we'd sleep under six inches of quilts.

Question: What did you like best about growing up back then?

Grandma: Everyone knew to pitch in and do his or her share. We never dreamed of complaining.

Question: What was discipline like one hundred years ago? If you were bad, what was a typical punishment?

Grandma: Mother used to go outside, find a tree and she'd break off a small branch to make into a switch. The branches from the little peach tree didn't hurt you much, but I do remember once it really hurt and I had welts from the switching. The switch must have come from some other tree because the little peach tree wouldn't have caused welts. I didn't resent the punishments because they were just part of growing up in a big family.

Question: Do you have advice for the younger members of the family?

Grandma: Today, it's harder to teach responsibility, but it's still important for each of you and for your future happiness. Offer to help your parents. Take on more responsibility. Do something extra to help with the house or the yard. Why? Because real self-esteem and real self-confidence come from knowing that you contribute more than you take.

Sample Questions

Let them talk. They'll go on the most beautiful journey that you won't get if you ask questions that are too specific.

- When and where were you born?
- Did you have brothers and sisters? How many? And where did you fit in the birth order?
- Did you have chores when you were young?
- What was something really different back then, something younger people would be surprised about?
- What did you like best about growing up back then?
- If you were bad, what was a typical punishment?
- Were you part of the family business when you were growing up?

- Do you have advice for the younger members of the family?
- What are the values you'd most like to see in the family now and in the future?
- What did you do for fun?
- What was school like for you?
- Tell us about your favorite friend?
- What's your earliest memory?
- What did you have for lunch?
- Who was your favorite teacher?
- What games did you play?
- Did the whole family play games?
- What was it like learning to drive?
- What was your first kiss?
- How long were you engaged?
- Describe your wedding?
- Who did you feel you could trust?
- Who would you go to when you were feeling bad?
- What kind of music did you listen to? And what was it played on?
- Did you have a pet?
- What was your favorite sport?
- Did you have a team that you cheered for?
- What were holidays like in your house?

Value Family Members,
Inside the Business or Not

Notes on Using This Newsletter

IN THE PERDUE FAMILY, WE OFTEN DESCRIBE THINGS AS "GLUEY" OR NOT "GLUEY." That refers to the concept we often use of "family glue," which means activities that promote family closeness. Frank was always particularly appreciative of things that were gluey.

Frank recognized the wisdom of the World War II expression that goes something like this: "We tend to be down on what we're not up on." He valued learning about each other because when we know each other, that is, when we're up on who we are and what we're doing, it's a powerful cultural factor for keeping us together as a family. Knowing about our family members is gluey.

PERDUE FAMILY NEWSLETTER

Dearest Family and Family Friends:

Here's s a quote from Pops from one of the old newsletters: "The most import-ant thing that we can do as a family is doing the things that will keep the family together over the generations."

In view of which, for future newsletters, I plan many interviews with family mem-bers and what they're up to. Today's is on Sara Nida, and the next one will focus on what Michael Oliviero is doing.

If you have a story or accomplishment you'd like included in a future Perdues' News, let me know. I can only write about what I hear about!

Love to all of you,

[signature]

Interview with Sara Nida

Question: You've managed to combine motherhood with a very successful career! Tell us about your career.

Sara: I've been lucky in my career because I love what I do and I love where I work, and I've had some incredible mentors along the way. I work for Estes, which is one of the largest LTL (Less-Than-Truckload) shipping companies. I work for their freight-forwarding division, and I began working for my division on the first day in 2003 when this division just began.

Back then, there were only five of us, while today it's 250 employees. In January of this year, I was promoted as VP of operations. By the way, my degree is in English so I'm a far cry from where I started, but I wouldn't have had it any other way.

Question: What is the Estes Company like?

Sara: It's a third-generation fami-ly-owned business founded 85 years ago. We employ almost 20,000 people, so Estes has a lot in common with Perdue. There is a culture of taking care of the employees just like you take care of your customers.

They know that if they don't have employ-ees, they don't have a business. Everyone is approachable; they're just good people, and very proud of their heritage. My boss Lance Harcrow is the best mentor a person could have, and I learn from him every day.

Question: Any clues on what Estes is doing right that helped it stay a highly successful family company?

Sara: Here are some of the things. We do a lot of promoting from within. Oh, and a big one is, we regularly do employee surveys to make sure that what we think of ourselves is accurate.

We also interview customers and vendors. Interestingly just about every response we get talks about the importance of the family culture. I'm proud of it. It comes from the very top down, that is from Rob Estes, the CEO.

Question: What about being a woman and a mother in an industry that historically hasn't exactly been a magnet for women?

Sara: It's been great. I know a lot of companies say they're family-oriented, but here we truly strive for work-life balance. Our senior VP and our CEO understand that sometimes a woman may need to take off early to pick up her child, and there's just no problem with this. There isn't a clock-out time. On the other hand, there are times when I've worked until 3:00 a.m. and sometimes I've needed to be away for a week. I like it that in this

company, I can be a role model for Alexa, and she can see that it's possible to be a mom and have a career.

Question: What does a typical workday look like for you?

Sara: On a typical day, I go to a lot of meetings. Today a lot of time was taken up making sure that some new transportation management software that's in beta is ready to go live in time for when our busiest time begins in spring.

Question: What is your dear husband up to?

Sara: We met working at Estes, but he's recently gotten his real estate license. Real estate gives him a lot of flexibility because if Alexa is sick or there's a snowstorm and the school is closed, Travis can take care of her. He's so great with kids.

Question: What is Alexa like, now that she's three?

Sara: She has the most fun little vocabulary. She put her hands over her eyes last night and told me, "Mommy, I disappeared!" For the most part, she's a happy-go-lucky, go-with-the-flow kind of child. She enjoys being around other kids, and the family trip will be wonderful for her.

Question: I bet everyone will love hearing about your career and how you can still be a fully-engaged mom at the same time! Thank you.

Sample Questions

- You've managed to combine motherhood with a very successful career! Tell us about your career.
- How do you balance work and the children?
- How come you didn't want to work in the family business?
- What is your dream job?
- What is the _____ Company like?
- Any clues on what the company you work for is is doing right that helped it stay a highly successful family company?
- What about being a woman and a mother in an industry that historically hasn't exactly been a magnet for women?
- How do you make time for your kids?
- How do you make time for your husband?
- How do you cope with sometimes feeling overwhelmed?
- What suggestions do you have for our company about how to be more family-oriented?
- Do you think our being family-oriented plays a big role in employee retention?
- What does a typical workday look like for you?
- What about _____? (Name of husband) What is he up to?
- What is(are) the birthday(s) of your child(children)?
- What is your daughter (or son or children) like?
- What do they enjoy doing?

Family Member Who's an Artist:
This Enriches Us All

Notes on Using This Newsletter

TODAY'S NEWSLETTER IS ON THE IMPORTANCE OF ART TO OUR FAMILY. THE SUBJECT of art is on my mind because of a conversation I had on the MegaBus, going from New York City to Boston. I sat beside a young Korean who's just graduated from college. Even though he grew up in Korea, he wants to live in New York City and become an American citizen.

His reason? He told me that in South Korea, the country has made astonishing strides economically, but they've put such an emphasis on science and technology that in his view, they've short-changed the artistic side of life. He values the artistic and cultural richness he finds in this country so much that he's expecting to give up his Korean nationality. He can't be happy without art.

This took my breath away. A young man would give up his country because art was so central to what made life enjoyable for him? I know he was only one person and he was only speaking for himself. Still, I took it to heart when I heard him say that the cultural side of life was critical to his happiness. That made me value all the more that our family has a vibrant cultural side.

How about your family and the arts? Do you have members who in one way or another add to the family's cultural dynamism? If so, celebrate them in a newsletter! Pick and choose from the questions that might apply to your family member and then share this cultural richness with the rest of your family.

PERDUE FAMILY NEWSLETTER

Dearest Family and Family Friends:

The arts have always been a strong point in this family. We are a business family, but family members also include musicians, artists, and art history majors who love to talk art. Today's issue is about Beverley Perdue Jennings' career. She's received national recognition, and we can all take pride in her achievements.

Love to all of you,

Interview with Beverley Perdue Jennings

Question: What gives you the impulse to paint?

Bev: The goal is to paint and in the process, to precipitate an image that simply must come out. It's as if there's an image inside that must be brought into existence, and sometimes I can push the right buttons and make it be seen.

Question: How does it feel when you are painting?

Bev: When things are going great, the feeling is wonderful. I can be painting and there are not enough hours in the day. I can be up painting till two or three in the morning. I paint best when I do it intuitively. However, when you're on location facing a blank piece of paper it takes a lot of self-confidence and instinct to "just do it." But when it's going well, nothing is better.

Question: You sometimes say a painting develops a life of its own.

Bev: It really does. That is, if you're lucky. You just grab hold and follow the message, or the spirit of the painting, which is what I did in that painting. Ralph and I say to each other, jokingly, "Our studio angels are at work."

Question: Tell us why you enjoy your chosen career.

Bev: I'm so grateful that I've had this door opened because it is something I can do forever. I get to meet the most wonderful people, especially the artists and buyers who become good friends.

Question: Do you enjoy talking with potential clients?

Bev: Many artists don't like selling and are afraid to talk to potential clients. I enjoy talking about a painting. For me, it's almost like a game. It's not the money, it's the challenge that I like when I'm selling the work.

Question: Is it ever emotionally hard for you to sell you work? Like you get attached to it?

Bev: I'm terrible about selling paintings, I'll refuse to sell certain ones because they're almost like my children.

Question: What was your first sale?

Bev: It was about 15 years ago and it was for $95. People saw some of my paintings in Bob's office, and someone made an offer. It was very flattering.

Question: You have had some impressive career successes recently. You've won several regional watercolor competitions, and in the last few days you've been accepted into a major show, the National Water Color Society Signature and Associate Member Exhibition at the Downey Museum of Art in California. This kind of recognition didn't just drop in your lap. What gave you the courage to start entering competitions?

Bev: It began when I was sitting next to an 83-year-old woman who told me, "Beverly, you need to start entering juried national and regional art shows around the country to get your name out. If I was younger, that's what I would do. Otherwise you'll always just be nothing more than a painter from Virginia."

I realized that she was right, but it was hard to get started. The problem is, it's hard even to be accepted to be part of the competition. In fact, many artists never enter shows and the biggest reason is that they fear rejection. In the Virginia Watercolor Show that I entered, I didn't get accepted until I had tried four times. The rejections were a challenge. Every time you get an envelope back from a competition that you are trying to enter, if the envelope has a slide in it, you know that you didn't get in. But once I started entering national shows four years ago, I got on a roll.

Question: How do you handle rejection and discouragement?

Bev: When I enter a show and get rejected, I tell myself, "Jurying is very subjective and it's just one person's opinion!" Or, "Maybe I got rejected because the slide I sent as a sample of my work wasn't good enough." When things happen, like I didn't get into the 1996 Southern Show even though I won it the year before, the message is, "Well, keep your feet on the ground and don't get carried away with yourself."

Question: Which show did you enter first?

Bev: I got into the Mid-Atlantic Watercolor Show in Baltimore and I got an award for it. I also got into the National, Midwest, Virginia, other shows around the country. Just getting into them was an award as far as I was concerned. It got so that I would get in the show and the second year I would get an award. In 1995, I got the Best in Show in the Southern Watercolor Society for my painting "A Spiritual Message." To be in a national magazine was hard to imagine. I was very lucky, and luck and timing are also part of the formula.

Question: Any final thoughts on your career as a professional artist?

Bev: Art is my identity. I'm always surprised at how many strangers know me by my art—and not as Frank Perdue's daughter. To create something that other people really like is extremely rewarding. I am so lucky because I get to live my bliss. As Joseph Campbell says, "Follow your bliss," and fortunately, I've found my bliss.

Sample Questions

- What gives you the impulse to paint?
- How does it feel when you are painting?
- I've included a photograph of one of your recent works. I really like it, but I don't know why I like it. Can you tell us about it?
- You sometimes say a painting develops a life of its own. Can you talk about what you mean by this?
- Why do you enjoy your career?
- Did anyone try to discourage you from your career as an artist?
- Who encouraged you to follow your dreams?
- Are most of your friends artists?
- What energizes you in your work?
- Who's your favorite artist?
- Other than today, what other artistic era speaks to you most?
- How did you learn your craft.
- What suggestions do you have for someone who's thinking about being an artist?

- How much discipline does it take?
- What's hardest for you about being an artist?
- At what age did you know you wanted to be an artist?
- How much do you gain energy from hanging out with artists?
- Do you enjoy talking with potential clients?
- Is it ever emotionally hard for you to sell your work? Do you get attached to it?
- What was your first sale?
- Have you ever entered competitions?
- How do you handle rejection and discouragement?
- What's your workday like?
- How have you arranged your studio?
- How do you handle interruptions (for example, a phone call)?
- Any final thoughts on being an artist?

Family Member Who's a Musician:
Adds to Our Cultural Heritage

Notes on Using This Newsletter

I MENTIONED IN A PREVIOUS NEWSLETTER HOW IMPORTANT IT IS TO CELEBRATE family members who are in the arts. The amount they contribute to the spiritual and emotional richness of the family makes their contribution priceless. Let's celebrate the family members who do so much for a family's soul.

If your family has poets, artists, musicians, or authors, celebrate them. In fact, I'd also celebrate family members who aspire to a career in the arts, just because they do so much to expand and nourish the family's identity. They're a huge part of "what makes us who we are."

PERDUE FAMILY NEWSLETTER

Dearest Family and Family Friends:

This is an amazingly creative family! As an example, consider G4, Mike Oliviero. He has my current nomination for "The Family Genius."

I've always loved his music and I've always been dazzled by his charisma and stage presence. I've just now visited his website and have been reading some of the testimonials for his work.

There are many to choose from, but how about this one!

"Mike Oliviero is a craftsperson of a rare, high order. His lines arise from a poet's eye and rise with a singer's ear. He shapes complex, dimensional music. And in the end, these precise, intellectual soundscapes break open and flood with thick emotion. I find his music endlessly engaging and deeply moving."
— Rob Seals, Founder,
The Songwriting School of Los Angeles

Or this one:

"Oliviero [Mike's group] are a force to be reckoned with. Mike, Donovan, Cara, and Dave are not afraid to push the boundaries of their sound and arrangements. Not conforming to tradition, structure, or form, they explore a wide range of dynamics, not just across the "If You're Going to Be a Bear" EP, but within the songs themselves. Textural and thought-provoking lyrics that really take you on a journey, keep you captivated and wanting more!
— Lynne Earls, Mixer/Engineer/Founder,
Earls Music Productions (KD Lang,
Bobby Bazini)

So, enjoy learning more about our gifted family member, Michael Oliviero!

Love to all of you

Interview with Mike Oliviero

Question: Tell us about what you're up to now.

Mike: Right now, we're working on a sequel to our recently released EP, "If You're Going to Be a Bear." It's for our next show at the Hotel Cafe on Sunday, April 24, at

8 pm. This is a step up for us, getting to perform at the Hotel Cafe.

We also have a tour coming up, from the end of April to the end of May. We'll be playing in several states including California, Washington, Oregon, New Mexico, Colorado, and Arizona.

Question: That sounds fantastic!

Mike: We're not making a lot of money, and the pay is about what I'd make during an eight-hour day in an office job. But even if the band isn't making a ton of money, we get to play music, and it's good for getting our name out there.

Question: How do you even find these venues?

Mike: Zé's girlfriend, the rock star Lezlie Deane, helped me with a massive list of them. It would have been hard to find this without Lezlie's help.

Question: For those who don't know, Lezlie is a former Hollywood actress who starred in numerous feature films and TV shows, toured the world with her band Fem2Fem, and is currently the lead singer of Scary Cherry And The Bang Bangs. Mike, to continue, what about your social life? Do you hang out with other musicians?

Mike: I'm beginning to build a network of local artists and one of the ways I do it is, I live in a warehouse that doubles as both living space and rehearsal space. The great thing about this is that we can have live music there. By doing shows in the warehouse, we can provide a place for people to enjoy art and music without having to pay for the space. People can make a donation, but they can also come for nothing. I'm kind of solitary in general, but this is a great way to begin building a network.

Question: Where can people buy your work?

Mike: Come to Apple's iTunes and hunt for "Oliviero." There are five songs available for 99 cents each. Or come to my website at www.OlivieroMusic.com/music/.

Sample Questions

Note for person writing this e-mail: There are questions for people at various levels in their careers. You'll probably need to ignore a bunch of questions that don't apply to your family musician.

- When did you start loving (*name the musical instrument or aspect of music that engages the family member such as voice or composing)?*

- What instrument do you play?
- Did you love it from the beginning?
- How much musical education did you have?
- Did one of your parents insist you practice a lot and then you learned to love it, or were you born loving it?
- How much time do you spend practicing?
- Tell us about what you're up to now musically.
- How do you feel about classical music?
- Who's your favorite contemporary composer?
- Who's your favorite classical composer?
- Is there a living musician whose life you particularly admire?
- Is there a musician from the past whose life you particularly admire?
- What genre do you most enjoy?
- What's most challenging to you in your musical development?
- Do you enjoy performing?
- How much do you enjoy composing?
- What does it feel like when you're composing?
- What does it feel like when you're practicing?
- What does it feel like when you're playing for friends?
- Is there a difference in how you feel between playing for family and friends and a paid engagement?
- Where do you get your inspiration for what you compose?
- A musician's life can be difficult. How do you cope?
- Who is your mentor?
- Is your family supportive of your being a musician?
- Do you need to have a day job in order to be a musician?
- I assume you're strongly auditory in your approach to life. Do you enjoy the visual world equally?
- What music do you listen to when you're not playing?
- Are you now doing this professionally? If not, is this something you want to do?
- How hard is it to find jobs?

Help Your Family Business Succeed across the Generations

Notes on Using This Newsletter

THIS ISSUE COMES ABOUT BECAUSE OF AN ARTICLE ON PRENUPTIAL AGREEMENTS I wrote for the Family Firm Institute's magazine, *The Practitioner* (https://ffipractitioner.org).

A reader, Thomas Waring, read the article and e-mailed me about the disasters that happen after family cultures mix because of marriage, but don't successfully blend.

We corresponded several times, and his e-mails got me to questioning how well families in general do in blending the in-laws and their families. It's an issue worth paying attention to.

Does your family have a successful plan to integrate the married-ins? Do you make them feel part of the team? Welcomed? Cherished? The sample newsletter text is unlikely to apply to your family situation, but it can start your thinking on this important topic.

PERDUE FAMILY NEWSLETTER

Dearest Family and Family Friends:

I think you'll agree that we're doing well in being welcoming to our married-ins. While no one is perfect, I think we're entitled to give ourselves something of a pat on the back. Read what married-in Keith Eliason says, and then figure out what we should do more of and what we can do better.

Love to all of you,

Keith

Interview with Keith Eliason

Question: How many years have you been married now?

Keith: It's been 20 years and it's been good. Every marriage has bumps in the road, but I wouldn't change a thing. It's been wonderful.

Question: What's it like marrying into a family like ours? Is it hard to find a balance between your own identity and being a member of the extended family?

Keith: It's not an issue because the rest of the family seems like an extension of my family. I never felt that I wasn't a part of the family. We've done so much together since the beginning that being members of the family is simply who we all are.

Question: Talk about your children and how they're doing.

Keith: Connor is sixteen and Sean is fourteen. They're both working toward being Eagles in Scouting. They're each one merit badge away from beginning their Eagle project.

Question: But I always thought you had to be a senior in high school to make Eagle. I can remember back in the 1940s my grandfather telling me that one of the most admirable things that could happen to an older boy is to become an Eagle Scout.

Keith: In our troop, we know that cars and girls will come into play, so we try to get boys to finish their Eagle projects by 16.

Question: What will their projects be?

Keith: There's a state camp ground near us and it needs some bridges and other upgrades so they're likely to work on something to do with upgrading the camp ground.

Question: What are the two boys like?

Keith: Connor likes to do physical work; Sean not so much. They both love hunting and fishing and both boys are incredible shots. Sean is a gifted hunter; he understands the things you must do to make things happen. Connor is equally awesome; he's physically strong, and he's always there to help other smaller kids. He's got that nice laid-back kind of personality to him, there's no arrogance.

Question: Fabulous. Switching gears, what values are you instilling in your children?

Keith: I think most values are there by the time they're seven. We wanted to teach them such things as: be honest; take care of your family; and if you say you're going to do something, do it.

Question: How do you deal with the possibility of substance abuse?

Keith: I've beat into them from the start that drugs are not what an intelligent person does. Doing drugs is a choice that someone who doesn't like himself makes. I've always encouraged them to think things through and make intelligent

choices and obviously doing drugs is not an intelligent choice in life.

Question: Any advice for family members who are thinking of getting married?

Keith: Don't rush, take your time, everybody thinks you can rush into things because you can rush out. But think of it as one-way, this-is-the-choice-you-make kind of decision. Is this the person for you, the one you can make a commitment to for the rest of your life? Make sure that you're ready, that you can afford to be married. If you can't take care of yourself, you're not ready to take care of a family.

Question: Switching subjects again, anything we should do to make it easier for married-ins when they first join?

Keith: We do a pretty good job as it is, so no need to fix anything. What we're good at is that we make everyone who joins the family feels as if they've always belonged.

We always show interest in the new person and it's almost like instant family. Further, we're a family that likes to be together. You hear of stories where everyone is fighting but for the most part we enjoy being together. It's who we are.

Question: In the Perdue family, we're always joking about in-laws and their families (we sometimes refer to them as "out-laws"). Is it funny or is there a "many a truth is said in jest" aspect to it? I can think of times when we have family photographs of everyone and then we have photographs of the in-laws and then the out-laws, and everyone is yelling about who is better, as if we're separate teams.

Keith: There's no edge to the in-laws and out-laws joking, it's all in good fun. When you're comfortable with a subject, you can joke about it.

Sample Questions

- How many years have you been married now?
- What's it like marrying into a family like ours? Is it hard to find a balance between your own identity and being a member of the extended family?
- Talk about your children and how they're doing.
- Talk about your career.
- What about recreation?
- What values are you instilling in your children?
- Do you have any advice for family members who are thinking of getting married?
- You have a home that people rave about. What's the story behind it?
- What do you find most exciting in your life right now?
- What are your memories of one of the older family members?
- Anything we should do to make it easier for married-ins when they first join?
- We're always joking about in-laws and out-laws. Is it funny or is there a "many a truth is said in jest" aspect to it?

Birth of a Child: We Cherish New Members

Notes on Using This Newsletter

THE BEST NEWSLETTERS EVER ARE ONES WHERE WE WELCOME NEW FAMILY MEMBERS. Sometimes a new member is joining us because of an engagement and sometimes it's because of the birth of a child.

I think we're all deeply wired to care about who is a member of our family and knowing the new members, even if it's only through a newsletter, means we know more about who we are and what makes us who we are.

I recommend a newsletter for the birth of every child. In the Henderson and the Perdue families, the newsletters on the birth of a child become not only introductions of the new family member, but the newsletters also become souvenirs over the years.

These newsletters are also wonderful to send out to family friends or maybe to the bridesmaids, ushers, ministers, and anyone who has an interest in the husband and wife.

PERDUE FAMILY NEWSLETTER

Dearest Family and Family Friends:

Today we are welcoming a very new member of the family, thirteen-days-old Jordan Viera Henderson. Enjoy the story of how Jordan became one of us!

Love to all of you,

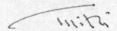

Interview with Annette Henderson

Question: Share with us what Jordan's birth was like!

Annette: He was stubbornly breech for most of the pregnancy but at thirty-six weeks one of the doctors felt that he had switched positions. This didn't last, because Jordan decided that he liked to be head up in the world. That raised the likelihood of a C-section.

C-sections can mean less risk to a breech baby because a normal delivery means the possibility of a cord prolapse or hip dysplasia. We looked into the options of trying to turn him, including my hanging upside down, acupuncture, and the Sa-domasochistic Princess Treatment which involves burning an incense stick near one of my little toes until it was uncomfortable and then switching to another toe.

We kept hoping that the baby would flip the last couple of days because this is what had happened with Tommy just before he was born. However, we scheduled a C-section for October 27th.

That isn't how it worked out. On Friday, the 21st, we went out for dinner. I was feeling some pain in my pelvis and assumed I had pulled something when walking earlier in the day. We weren't expecting the baby for another week and were thinking we'd be chilling out for a week. But at dinner the pain was coming back. I had no idea that what I was experiencing was labor pains. We came home and started watching a movie.

Tommy asked me, "We're not having a baby tonight, are we?" I assured him, "No." But then the pains started to become regular. I began timing them and then, when I went to the bathroom, my water broke.

We rushed to the hospital. The doctor strapped me down, inserted an IV and told me, "In 45 minutes you're going to be holding your baby in your arms."

Jordan was born at 3:16 am, and the time it took from strapping on the IVs and starting the incision to being fully stitched up was 40 minutes. I was grateful for experiencing labor for a little while. When the contractions were two minutes apart, they weren't so terrible, but once they stopped allowing me to move it really hurt and I was ready for a spinal block.

Jordan was 6 pounds 3 ounces, 20 inches. Shortly after he was born, they put him on my chest, and then on Tommy's chest, and there he was, rooting through Tommy's chest hair looking to nurse.

The current thinking is it's good to have "skin on skin," because it helps with heartbeat and temperature regulation. He was also nursing within minutes of being born. They like to have the baby breastfeed within an hour.

Question: What is it like recovering from a C-section?

Annette: I stayed in the hospital from early Saturday morning until Tuesday.

It was great to have advice from Janie Henderson because she had experienced C-sections with her children.

She was wonderful talking me through it, reassuring me that I could care for Jordan. I was up walking within 8 hours of the surgery, and now I can walk two to three hours a day.

Question: Tell us about the name.

Annette: We didn't completely plan the name because we didn't want to know the gender of the baby ahead of time. Our thinking was, "There aren't that many anticipated good surprises and we didn't care whether it's a boy or a girl because anything is good for us."

When Jordan was born, we hadn't settled on a name for him so we were trying out names. He was Grayson for 8 hours. Then at 2:00 am, we tried on "Jordan" and it was clear to us that this was his name!

Question: Do you have any theories on child-rearing?

Annette: We're trying to be strict but loving at the same time. As every parent knows, it's a balancing act.

Sample Questions

- What was the pregnancy like?
- What was the birth like?
- What did the child weigh?
- What are your feelings on breastfeeding?
- How are you recovering from your C-section?
- Tell us about the name. Where did the first, middle, and last names come from?
- Do you have any theories on child-rearing, such as how strict you'll be?
- Did she arrive close to her due date?
- What is she like? (Easygoing? Sensitive? A lot of work?)
- How are her siblings handling it?
- What's best about having a family with more than one child?
- Do you have any advice for parents-to-be?
- Do you have help?
- Is the family dog OK with the new arrival?
- How did you introduce the baby to her siblings?

Family Member Wins an Award:
It's As if It Happens to Us All

Notes on Using This Newsletter

THERE ARE ALL SORTS OF DEFINITIONS OF FAMILY, AND I THINK WE'RE FREE TO pick the ones that work for us. Nevertheless, here's one I recommend. It's a way of distinguishing how we feel about each other, as opposed to how we feel about the people who are classmates or who work in an office.

The definition that I'm liking right now is that families are composed of lifelong associates who are an extension of "me" that lasts throughout our lives. If someone at the office has something good happen, we can be pleased and delighted, and maybe we care deeply. But it's different when a sister or cousin has something good happen; in a close family, it's as if when something happens to a member of the family, it happened to a part of you.

In a family, the distinction between you and others isn't a totally firm line. The line gets blurred or even blended, depending on how close you are as a family. That is why I like celebrating awards in family newsletters. An award is something good that happened to all of us.

PERDUE FAMILY NEWSLETTER

Dearest Family and Family Friends:

In a family, when one member does well, it reflects on all of us. That's part of what being a family means. It's something to celebrate and feel proud about.

Looking at it this way, we can all feel proud that our own Laura Williams achieved something wonderful.

Enjoy hearing about Laura's achieving the Girl Scout Gold Award!

Love to all of you,

Laura Williams Wins Girl Scout Gold Award

Mitzi: What is the Girl Scout Gold Award?

Laura: It's the equivalent of becoming an Eagle Scout. You have to work for 50 hours on your project, but I ended up doing 300 hours. You need a project you love because otherwise you won't do a great job with it. Only 7% of Girl Scouts ever get the Gold Award.

Question: Tell us about your project:

Laura: It began for me when in 10th grade. I saw a newsletter about a mission trip to the Hou Kola Learning Camp for the Lakota Indian tribe in South Dakota. Twenty people were going to the reservation for a week of tutoring native American elementary-age children in the summer.

Question: So, you got to be a member of this group? I imagine there was a real need for this tutoring?

Laura: Where we were going were the two poorest counties in the United States. There are many suicides, 80% unemployment, and the dropout rate before graduating is 70%.

Question: How did you prepare for the project?

Laura: I asked the kids at the Vacation Bible School at my church to help me collect money that would be used to provide school supplies for 52 Lakota children. The supplies were for the kids to have for the next school year. By the last day of Bible School, I had enough to buy supplies and backpacks for each child.

Question: What was your job once you were at the reservation?

Laura: I was a counselor and got to teach the children such things as reading, math, writing, technology, and art.

Question: What are your plans for the future?

Laura: I'm interested in psychology, or social work, or maybe medicine.

Sample Questions

- What is the award you just won?
- How did you get interested in competing for it?
- Why did you feel there was a need for it?
- How did you prepare for the project?
- What did you do?
- What happened afterwards?
- What did you learn from it?
- Are you a different person as a result?
- What was the biggest satisfaction?How does it feel to have won this honor?
- What are your plans for the future?

Our Family Vacation: A Major Deposit in the Bank of Family Closeness

Notes on Using This Newsletter

ONE OF THE BIG LESSONS, AS BRIGHT AS ALL THE GLITTERING LIGHTS ON BROADWAY, is that families need to spend time together if they're to achieve their fullest bonding. It's spending time together that results in shared memories and aligning of attitudes and values. In the Henderson family, we've been doing this since 1890, and the Perdue family has been doing this even before 1920, when the family business started.

The Henderson get-togethers began when my great-great-grandfather endowed the Henderson Estate Dinners back in 1890. Likewise, Frank endowed vacations to make sure we'd stay together as a family.

This newsletter is a report of a recent vacation. If you choose to write about a vacation, I imagine that every word in your newsletter will be different from the newsletter you'll see here. But the questions can help you get started, and the sample text will show how we handled a newsletter on a family vacation.

PERDUE FAMILY NEWSLETTER

Dearest Family and Family Friends:

We are so lucky that Pops made it possible for all of us to be together for a family vacation once every eighteen months. Vacations are not only a time for fun and fellowship and learning, they're one of the most important factors that help keep us together as a family. Shared experiences and shared knowledge help strengthen the culture that makes us a family. We owe such a debt of gratitude to Pops for having the foresight to make these family bonding activities possible.

Family member Keith Eliason and Zé Ayala oversaw arranging this year's vacation. A big thank-you to both men for doing this. We all know that it takes more time than any of us can easily guess to figure out a time that we can all make it, and then book the hotels, tours, activities, and everything else that goes into making a successful family vacation.

The fact that we had a great location and a great time isn't something that was guaranteed to happen. By the time we had all decided on a Western vacation, there were no resorts that could handle a group our size that weren't already booked and that could accommodate the budget we had.

Honest, I was several times ready to give up, but Zé kept trying and finally he heard about Lone Mountain Ranch. It turned out to be a fabulous find, with fly fishing, hiking, mountain biking, trail rides, nature hikes, canoeing, and probably ten other things I've forgotten.

A highlight of the trip was our July 12th visit to Yellowstone National Park. We saw Old Faithful erupt, saw Painted Pot boiling hot springs, and heard a lecture on why the forest recovers slowly from fires: The growing season has only sixty consecutive days without freezing temperatures, and there's only ten inches of rain each year.

Another very important part of our time together was listening to family relationship specialist Wanda Ortwine. She stated that no relationship can survive without trust, honesty, and communication.

"If you lose one of those," she emphasized, "the relationship may be over before it can be repaired."

Because of the importance of trust, honesty, and communication, she said families need to deal with issues while they're small. She recommends recognizing that being right is far less important than being understanding.

Something else she emphasized: people sometimes have the choice between "being right" and having a relationship. Being addicted to "being right" can be destructive in a family.

Family cultures need to help people avoid this dangerous addiction, the addiction to being right.

We asked Wanda her view of successful family relationships. Her answer, which seemed good to the rest of us, was: people get along with each other and help each other be all they can be in a way that supports the group, as well as the individual.

Personally, I think that nails it. However, Wanda warns that for all families, achieving this goal takes time. People need to go slow to go fast.

Love to all of you,

Sample Questions

- How did you choose this location?
- What were the amenities you were most looking for?
- Did you make any special arrangements such as babysitting or kid-friendly activities so family members with younger children would particularly enjoy it?
- Ideally, how far ahead of time should we make our decision about where to go, in order to get the best reservations?
- What was the best part of the trip?
- From the point-of-view of family closeness, what worked best?
- What should we change for future years?
- How important are these trips for keeping our family together?
- Is it worthwhile to have someone come talk with us about family dynamics?
- How do we feel about the tension between "being right" and having a relationship?
- What does a successful family relationship look like?
- What was your budget for the trip?

- How is this paid for?
- What is the incentive to have the family members come?
- What are the requirements for nonfamily members to come? Do they need to be engaged? Or close to engaged? Or have a very long relationship? Or, are all family members with significant others welcome to bring their significant others?

A Serious Illness: A Model for Grace, Courage, and Acceptance

Notes on Using This Newsletter

FOR FAMILIES TO ENDURE, THEY NEED TO FACE WHAT THE TRADITIONAL WEDDING vows have said in countless ceremonies across millennia: they need to be there for each other "in sickness and in health." Family members need to know how family members deal with serious illness. It's a chance for learning life lessons about bravery, courage, and grace. This is something not to be shied away from.

Your newsletters will be entirely different from mine about Pops/Frank. But writing your own version of it is a worthy effort in teaching family members "how we do things." In the case of Pops, I consider the lessons he taught were almost celestial. As you'll read in the newsletter, when I asked him how he felt about being diagnosed with Parkinson's, there wasn't a single moment of "Poor me!" Rather, it was gratitude for all the years he didn't have it.

Good luck with whatever illness you are writing about. May it turn out to be not as bad as you feared. But if it does turn out in ways that you wish were different, at least you have a chance to model how people do handle with grace, courage, and resilience the blows life delivers to all of us. It's a priceless lesson.

PERDUE FAMILY NEWSLETTER

Dearest Family and Family Friends:

This newsletter contains some medium-bad news, but it could be a lot worse and there are some very big pluses involved.

Pops has been diagnosed with Parkinson's Disease, the same disease that Michael J. Fox has. It's in its very early stages, and Dr. Reich assures us all that it will not shorten Frank's life in any way.

Further, the medication that treats Parkinson's is very good at the beginning stages. It can help ward off trembling, swallowing difficulties, and problems with walking. The medication is problematic for younger people, like Michael J. Fox, because with them, after seven to fifteen years, the medications that are available begin to lose efficacy.

With people seventy and older, the medication usually work well as long as it's needed, and besides, there are new medications coming on that may last even longer. Popls is lucky to have gotten the disease at eighty-two.

You may wonder how there can be any pluses with a nasty disease like Parkinson's The pluses are that the medications do work and can be the answer to some gnawing problems Pops has been having.

He's better off having a treatable illness, than having symptoms that we don't know the cause of and can't do anything about.

Love to all of you,

Interview with Pops

Question: How do you feel about having been diagnosed with Parkinson's Disease?

Pops: *C'est la vie*, that's life. I'm thankful for all the years that I didn't have it.

Question: You think it will slow you down?

Pops: It already has.

Question: What's the worst thing about it?

Pops: My inability to be as active as I would like to be.

Question: Your father enjoyed life when he was in his 80s and 90s and couldn't be very active. What did he like to do at those ages?

Pops: He enjoyed flowers, particularly amaryllis and roses. He'd get the bulbs for the amaryllis from the nursery in Pittsville, and on Sundays he always wore a rose that he had grown himself.

Question: Could you ever get into growing flowers?

Pops: No. (Said with emphasis.)

Question: What do you enjoy most now?

Pops: I enjoy watching sports, I enjoy the local baseball team and I go to a lot of their games. I enjoy movies. In the past, I used to write down in my little book which movies won the Academy Awards each year. I thought that I would rather see the most popular ones than the unpopular ones. That's how I happened to see some of my favorite movies, such as the "Guns of Navarone."

I also like watching the History Channel, World War II shows in particular, but also the Civil War, and Ancient Egypt if it's about Cleopatra. Since I can no longer read, I very much enjoy listening to books on tape. I think I've listened to most of the books that exist on tape having to do with the Founding Fathers. I've also listened to everything I can find by David McCullough.

Question: I notice that most days you exercise an hour a day on the treadmill and sometimes even more. Do you do it because you enjoy it or because you feel you ought to?

Pops: I do it because people should exercise. I do not enjoy it.

Question: What do you wish for your grandchildren and great-grandchildren?

Pops: I wish that they would develop ways of solving the problems that will inevitably come up so they can all get along and be both productive citizens and good citizens.

Love to all of you,

Sample Questions

- How do you feel about having been diagnosed with _____?
- How much is it slowing you down?
- What's the worst thing about it?
- Your father enjoyed life when he was in his 80s and 90s and couldn't be very active. What did he like to do at those ages?
- What do you enjoy most now?
- I notice that most days you exercise an hour a day on the treadmill and sometimes even more. Do you do it because you enjoy it or because you feel you ought to?
- What do you wish for your grandchildren and great-grandchildren?
- Do you have any advice for them about money? I notice that you always live way, way below your means and that one of the greatest compliments you can give someone is, "She's tight as the bark on an oak tree."
- What are you doing to get your affairs in order?
- How do you feel about being public about your illness?
- What are doing to help your family members feel comfortable interacting with you now?
- If it hard for you to talk about it?
- Are there things you wish your family knew and might not know?
- Have you made your medical care wishes known?
- How do you feel about a final directive?
- What was the best thing about your life?
- What's your prognosis? Do you feel shy discussing these things?
- Has anything positive come out of this?
- Have you made any life changes because of this?
- Do you view the world differently?
- Do you feel up to visitors or do you prefer being left alone?
- Do you enjoy getting flowers? If yes, fresh flowers or plants?
- Would you prefer books, puzzles, books-on-tape, or videos?
- Was there anything you could have done to prevent it?
- What has this illness taught you about life?

A Family Member and Surgery:
Get the News Right and Avoid Rumors

Notes on Using This Newsletter

I'M GUESSING YOU'RE LOOKING AT THIS SAMPLE NEWSLETTER BECAUSE SOMEONE in your family has had surgery. The family will want to know about it, and knowing what's going on brings the family together when sharing an experience.

It's also important to get accurate information rather than getting it third-hand. You may want to do this as an email update. Make sure that you have the permission of your family member before sending out the information. Some family members may be very private about this kind of information, so out of courtesy be careful to check.

PERDUE FAMILY NEWSLETTER

Dearest Family and Family Friends:

I know you'll want an update on how Pops's heart surgery went. Basically, he's doing very well now. The anesthesiologist told me afterwards that everyone in the entire operating room was amazed at the strength of his heart. He had an extremely steady beat that didn't speed up under stress, but instead simply beat more efficiently. That's what you'd expect of a trained athlete, such as a marathoner, according to the anesthesiologist.

Also, something that you might enjoy knowing about Pops. The morning of the operation, I got to walk beside the gurney as he was being wheeled towards the operating theater, I asked him on a scale of one-to-ten how nervous he felt. His answer was "Two." He added, "You got to do what you got to do. It's like another day at the office." And this was not a case of his being in denial. He had talked at length the day before about things that he would want carried out if the operation did not go well.

When he got out of surgery, I had been warned that he might have "cognitive deficit" and not really be yourself or remember things well for as much as six months. When he woke up and could first talk, the intensive-care nurse asked if he could tell who he was, the date, and who was president. He was fine with who he was and what the date was, but when it came to who was president, the answer was, "Arkansas…." and for a moment I was bracing for cognitive deficit, until he finished the thought, "yes, the man from Arkansas, Bill Clinton." I learned afterwards that it was brilliant of him to wake up from so much drugs and still be so alert.The first five days of his recovery went well. He never needed the strong painkillers that you can give yourself intravenously. Tylenol was sufficient to control his pain.

During this period, the floor nurse told me that five days into surgery, most heart patients have no interest in the outside world. Pops was keenly interested in the evening news and during the day, we often watched the Ken Burns series on baseball. I think I remember that there were twenty-three hours of them and we watched them all.

Well, that's how things stand. He's home now and doing well. The doctors say he shouldn't drive for four to five weeks after the surgery and the tape we saw from Johns Hopkins about how to handle convalescence says that he shouldn't go back to work for three months. Somehow I don't think Pops will stick to that.

My doubts about his not being willing to stick to the rule increased when yesterday, the day he was released from the hospital, he decided to stop by the office "for just a few minutes" to have a look at his desk. He said he'd start the period of being away from the office after this one little exception.

That's our Pops!

Love to all of you,

Smith

Sample Questions

- Why did our relative need major surgery?
- Was it sudden or expected?
- Was it a complete or partial success?
- What's the prognosis?
- Do you have any technical details about the operation?
- Are the medications handling the pain?
- What's his/her attitude about pain medications?
- How is his/her morale?
- Is he/she taking an interest in things?
- Is he/she enjoying TV or books? What TV? Which books?
- Does he/she want visitors?
- Does he/she want flower or fruit baskets?
- Is she/he following doctor's orders? That is, is he/she a good patient?
- What restrictions is he/she up against?
- Will there be rehab or physical therapy?
- Is he/she being courageous about it?
- Did anything funny or memorable happen because of the surgery?
- What's the surgeon's name?
- What will change in his/her life?

Eulogy: How We Honor and Remember Family Members Who Have Gone Before

Notes on Using This Newsletter

FUNERALS ARE OF COURSE AN INEVITABLE PART OF LIFE. THEY BELONG IN YOUR newsletters also. They're part of your family's history, they're comforting to all, and they're helpful if there are family members who couldn't make it to the funeral.

This is a fairly easy newsletter to write—or at least the writing part of it is easy, because all you need to do is print the actual eulogy. Be sure to get a copy for your newsletter.

The hard part is that your heart may be breaking. But here's something that just may be a comfort to you. It comes from Thornton Wilder, the great Peterboro, New Hampshire, playwright who wrote the play "Our Town." He said, "The greatest tribute to the dead is not grief, but gratitude." A eulogy is an expression of gratitude for a person's life. Embrace it. Share it.

Future generations will be grateful.

And meanwhile, my sympathies for what you're going through. This is not an easy time.

PERDUE FAMILY NEWSLETTER

Dearest Family,

It is with overwhelming sadness that we record the passing of Mary Ellen Sirman.

What a fabulous part of our family life she was! I always loved her equanimity. I can remember her as Rock of Gibraltar at our Thanksgiving celebrations.

People might be upset about what was going on geopolitically or whatever else was looming in our lives, and she always, with a few calming words, would always put everything in perspective. She allowed us to see that the external things were tangential, and our family relationships are what are centrally important. How we'll miss her!

For those of you who were not able to attend her funeral, and also for the many of you who did, I'm including an excerpt from her eulogy. In addition, it's a way of having a record of her life for future generations.

Love to all of you,

Eulogy of Mary Ellen Sirman

Every Christmas, Aunt Mary made cookies a full month ahead of time. We all received our box along with all of her friends and relatives, and there were a lot of them. She made fifteen different varieties, many of which were decorated for Christmas.

Aunt Mary's memory was so keen that just a few years ago, she told Beverly that she wanted a painting of Piney Grove where her grandfather ran a sawmill and lived near Mt. Olive Church.

She explained, in incredible detail, the country store that carried everything from furniture to nuts and bolts and, with an infectious smile, the wonderful candy! There was a sawmill, granary, a twenty-stall barn for the mules, and horses for the lumber operation. She even described a three-seated carriage with the fringe on top.

Aunt Mary described the two gardens, one for vegetables and the other for flowers. She described where the hog pen was. She even remembered where the hammock was! She drew a sketch for Bev and that sketching and the resulting painting are framed and hanging today in her little apartment that Bill so wonderfully fixed up for her when they left the farm.

Aunt Mary's beauty lies in her simplicity, developed from years of hard work and watching the work of the Lord unfold around her.

As Sandy said, "She had a wonderful simplicity of faith in her Lord Jesus that came through in everyday life." Aunt Mary never had a lot to say, especially about herself, but when she did speak, people wanted to hear what she had to say.

Anne tells the story of just a few years ago when she asked Aunt Mary what technological innovation, over the near century that Aunt Mary had lived, made the biggest impression on her and, with just a slight hesitation, Aunt Mary responded, "Indoor plumbing!"

Many of us today who may seem sophisticated in an increasingly complex world should take note of Aunt Mary's simplicity.

This is indeed both a sad occasion and a time to celebrate the life of a wonderful person. We will miss Aunt Mary.

Sample Questions

If you're going to write a eulogy, as opposed to using one that someone else has written, you might consider these questions, and then add ones that particularly apply to your loved one.

- When was he/she born?
- When did he/she pass?
- What took him or her?
- Who does he/she leave behind?
- What about his/her faith?
- What is a favorite memory of the deceased?
- Were holidays were important?
- What were his/her hobbies?
- What was the most wonderful/beautiful/touching aspect of his/her life?
- Are there any humorous stories about him/her?

Index

"love bombing," 75

malware, 68
marketing, 54
married-ins, integrating in family, 137–140
math, role in business, 86
McCauley, Jim, 63–66
McEvily, Justin, 23
mediation, 31
Mendoza, Drew, 14
mission, of family, 25–27
monetary success, problems with, 19
musician, family member as, 133–136

next generation, consideration for, 117
new skills, learning, 60–61
newsletters,
    distribution, 10
    editing, 9
    topics, 8-9
Nida, Sara, 125–126

Oliviero (group), 134–135
Oliviero, Anne, 37–38
Oliviero, Mike, 134–135
Opal Financial Group, Family Office &
    Private Wealth Conference, 23
Ortwine, Wanda, 149–150

parent, successful, problems with, 20, 22
Parkinson's Disease, 153
people skills, importance of, 60–61
Perdue, Chris, 105–106
Perdue family, 3, 148
Perdue Family Newsletters, origin, 4–5
Perdue Farms, business, 3
    advancement, family, 50–52
    Agri-Business, 105–106
    environmental sustainability, 95–99

fleet, 85–86
Headquarters building, 96–98
Inventory Management, Dept.,
    105–106
North Carolina floods, 39–42
performance, family, 50–52
Purchasing, Dept., 96–98
recognition, importance of, 108–110
response to crisis, 39–42
solar panel field, 96–98
Transportation, Dept., 85–86
Perdue, Frank, biographical details, 39–42,
    57–58, 89–90, 109–110, 153–154, 157–
    158
Perdue, Frank, biography (see *Tough Man,
    Tender Chicken*)
Perdue, Jim, 104
personal security, 62–66
    defending yourself, in attack, 65, 66
    eye contact, danger of, 64, 66
    locking doors, 64, 66
    rear end collision, danger of, 64, 66
    swindles, 65, 66
    vans, danger of, 63–64, 66
    vehicular hijacking, 64–65, 66
philanthropy (*see charitable giving*)
prenuptial agreements, 111–114, 137
pressure to perform, in family, 19
principles, 23–27
purpose, of family, 26

quarrels, 13, 28–31, 39

ransomware, 67–71
relationship problems, 2
reliability, 26–27
Rhoades, Kelton, Dr., 74
rumors, avoiding, 156–158

Made in the USA
Middletown, DE
03 November 2020